the mezzo cookbook

with john torode

£9.99
4/09 ⑤

the Mezzo cookbook

with **john torode**

by john torode and sarah francis
introduction by terence conran

recipe photography by james murphy
ingredients photography by diana miller

conran
OCTOPUS

First published in 1997 by
Conran Octopus Limited
37 Shelton Street
London WC2H 9HN

ISBN 1 85029 922 6

Recipes copyright © John Torode 1997
Non-recipe text copyright © Sarah Francis 1997
Design and layout copyright © Conran Octopus Ltd 1997
Recipe photography copyright © James Murphy 1997
Ingredients photography copyright © Diana Miller 1997

All rights reserved. No part of this book may be reproduced,
stored in a retrieval system, or transmitted, in any form or by
any means, electronic, electrostatic, magnetic tape,
mechanical, photocopying, recording or otherwise, without
prior permission in writing of the Publisher.

The right of John Torode and Sarah Francis to be identified as
Authors of the text of this Work have been asserted by them in
accordance with the Copyright, Designs and Patents Act 1988

Editorial Director: Suzannah Gough
Project Editor: Kate Bell
Editorial Assistant: Tanya Robinson
Copy Editor: Alexa Stace
Art Direction: Helen Lewis and Foundation Graphic Corp.
Design: Foundation Graphic Corp.
Stylist: Wei Tang
Production: Suzanne Bayliss and Jill Beed

British Library Cataloguing-in-Publication Data
A catalogue record for this book is available from the British Library

Printed and bound in China

Both metric and imperial measurements are given in the
recipes in this book. Use either all metric or all imperial as the
two are not necessarily interchangeable.

Page 2: mushroom tortellini
Page 5: (left to right) pink pickled ginger, making mushroom tortellini,
lemon mascarpone cake.
Pages 6–7: photographs of Mezzo by David Brittain.

contents

introduction

Mezzo is often described as the largest restaurant in Europe. In fact, it's a collection of complementary, food-related activities that we have gathered together under one enormous roof in the heart of Soho. Mezzo includes Soho's only bakery, a patisserie, café and four bars, as well as two very different restaurants. Upstairs, in Mezzonine, the menu has a distinctly Oriental twist: big bowls of Sweet Soy Noodles with Coriander, for example, or Vietnamese Vegetable Rolls in Rice Paper. The food is expertly prepared and quickly cooked, allowing people who pop in for a drink at the bar to stay for a meal ... after which many of them return to drinking!

Downstairs in Mezzo Restaurant, the pace is more leisurely, the food a fusion of East and West, northern and southern hemispheres. John Torode, Mezzo's wonderfully talented chef, has a real passion for mixing ingredients with expert flair and innovation. Here you'll find truly delicious food such as Potato and Thyme Rösti with Onion and Rocket, Seared Scallops with Green Mango, Grilled Sea Bream with Aubergine and Anchovies, and Fillet of Beef with Bone Marrow and Parmesan. People with a sweet tooth always make sure they save room for the terrific puddings.

Time and time again, Mezzo gives me a real buzz when I go there. The atmosphere is vibrant and energetic, there's always more than a sprinkling of glamour, and the food is a treat. We wanted to bring something that was new and exciting to Soho, whilst staying true to the character of a part of London that is celebrated for its cosmopolitan free spirit. At any time you can expect to see locals and tourists, the young and the not-so-young drinking and eating and chatting and enjoying themselves. What more could you or I hope for?

Terence Conran.

key ingredients

In recent years, cooking in the West has become increasingly adventurous, reaching out towards different cultures and cuisines, and adopting many of their styles and flavours for its own. Traditional recipes from Thailand, Malaysia, Japan, Korea, China, Italy and France have been plundered and reworked to create a type of cooking known variously as Pacific Rim, Mediterrasian, or, perhaps more accurately considering the process, Fusion. At Mezzo, such variety and innovation are central to our whole approach, and with every new season different ingredients are brought on board and incorporated in the creation of a constantly changing menu.

The discovery and promotion of new produce are essential to such experimentation: foods such as tamarind, palm sugar, coconut milk and lemon grass, integral to the cooking of Asia and the East, are slowly becoming more widely available in the West, and most supermarkets now boast shelves devoted specifically to these once unfamiliar items. This chapter provides a reference for such shelves, explaining exactly what it is you are looking for, and, if your supermarket is slow to catch on, where else you might find it. So don't be intimidated by the quest for new ingredients – whole new worlds open up to the domestic cook with every bag of lime leaves or bunch of bok choi. Cooking has never been such fun.

galangal

key ingredients

banana leaf

Large, glossy green leaves, slightly ribbed, from the banana tree. Available fresh from specialist supermarkets or florists, they are used in Thai and Far Eastern cuisine as an attractive means of presentation, with the food served either on the leaf, or wrapped up inside it.

beansprout

The sprouts of the mung bean. Beansprouts can be eaten either raw or cooked, and are often included in noodle dishes.

bok choi

A leafy green with sturdy white stems. Bok choi is one of the best-known Chinese vegetables, its name in Cantonese meaning, quite simply, 'white vegetable'. An ingredient in many soups, and noodle and dumpling dishes, bok choi should be bought fresh and used immediately.

cèpes (porcini)

Boletus edulis, cèpes or porcini, are wild mushrooms found in woodland clearings, generally under beech or coniferous trees, in late summer and autumn. They can be distinguished by their stout stalks, round tops, and the vertical tubes underneath the cap in which brown spores are produced. They have a deep, rich flavour and are widely available in fresh, dried and powdered forms. They are used in soups, stews and sauces.

chilli

A member of the sweet pepper (capsicum) family, there are hundreds of different varieties, from the fairly mild Anaheim to the tiny, very hot Thai or bird's-eye chillies. The seeds and core are the hottest parts of a chilli, and are normally removed unless you like your food very fiery. Always handle chillies with care and wash your hands after cutting them – chilli juice can be an extreme irritant.

choi sum

Also known as Chinese flowering cabbage, for obvious reasons, choi sum has tender green stems and yellow flowers, and can be boiled, steamed and stir-fried. It has a delicious flavour. Its name translates as 'vegetable heart', and the sweetest part of a choi sum is indeed the central leaves.

coconut

Coconut milk To make coconut milk, grate the flesh of a fresh coconut into a bowl and pour on 900ml/1½ pints/3½ cups of boiling water. Leave to stand for 10 minutes, then strain twice through a muslin-lined sieve, pressing down hard with a wooden spoon to extract all the milk. For thin coconut milk, skim off the cream on top. This will yield 600ml/1 pint/2½ cups of coconut milk. It is also available in cans, the best containing 17–19 per cent fat.

Coconut cream is skimmed from the top of coconut milk once the flesh has been pressed, as above. It is also available in blocks. The fat comes away in block form, and can be scraped off and used separately.

coriander

A member of the carrot family, coriander (also known as Chinese parsley, cilantro or pak chee) has a fresh, almost orange-like flavour and a lacy leaf similar in appearance to flat-leaf parsley. The leaves are used extensively in Thai and Oriental cooking for flavour and as a garnish, but the roots are also intensely aromatic, and are often used in Oriental soups and curries.

dashl

A light fish stock, made from dried bonito flakes (katsuobushi) and seaweed (konbu), that forms the basis of many Japanese soups. It can also be bought in powder form, to which water is added.

dried shrimp

Small, dried, red Asian shrimps, used in Oriental chillies, stir-fries and pastes. They are often toasted to bring out the flavour.

fish sauce

Derived from fermented fish or seafood, this bottled sauce is the basic seasoning used in most Thai cooking. Often extremely salty, its flavour changes according to the origin of the sauce, which ranges from anchovy, to prawn, crab, fish or squid. At Mezzo, the Squid brand is preferred.

galangal

A rhizome related to ginger, bought in root form and peeled, sliced and crushed before using. It has a sour flavour, with a faint smell of camphor, and is unmistakable when used in Thai curries and soups.

gelatine

A transparent, protein-based substance, derived from the boiling of beef bones, cartilage and tendons. Particularly useful in the making of jellies, puddings or terrines. Gelatine comes in leaf or powder form, but at Mezzo we prefer leaf as it is more stable. Leaf gelatine comes in three grades: gold, silver and bronze, with gold leaf being the best. Use according to pack instructions.

For a vegetarian alternative, use agar agar, which is available in most health food shops.

ginger

Native to South-East Asia, ginger root grows on an underground stem and, when fresh, has a pale, shiny skin that should be peeled before use. The flavour is both sharp and fresh tasting. Ginger is now widely available – look for large, smooth roots. Do not use powdered or dried ginger as a substitute.

hoisin sauce

A garlicky bean sauce made from soya beans, and often seasoned with chilli. Usually firm and sticky in texture, it is available in cans and jars from Chinese grocers and supermarkets.

kaffir lime and leaves

A smaller, more perfumed variety of lime. The rind is pungent in flavour and is an essential ingredient in curry pastes. The leaves are similarly aromatic, but can be bitter if used in large quantities. Kaffir leaves are occasionally difficult to find, but the fresh leaves can be replaced with dried or frozen if necessary.

lardons

Pieces of bacon or pancetta, approximately 1 x 4cm/½ x 1½in in size, cut crosswise to the rasher. Lardons are especially good when fried and added to salads or pasta dishes.

lemon grass

An aromatic herb, originating in South-East Asia. Lemon grass has a strong citrus flavour and long, grass-like leaves. The outer layers should be peeled, then the white part of the stem chopped or sliced. Avoid the woodier green tips of the stalk as these are tough and inedible.

lime pickle

A hot pickle made from the lime fruit, used widely in Indian cuisine, and available in most supermarkets.

maltose

A complex sugar available from Asian supermarkets and delicatessens. Maltose is used for roasting Peking duck (page 218). Honey can be used as a substitute if it is first boiled until reduced by about one-third.

mibuna

A Japanese salad leaf, increasingly available in delicatessens and specialist grocers.

mirin

A sweet form of Japanese rice wine, made from sake boiled with sugar.

miso

A bean paste made from fermented soya beans, miso is used widely in Japanese cooking as a soup and as a seasoning for stir-fries, and also sweetened, as cake. Aka-miso is red and lightly salted; sendai-miso is also red, but heavily salted; shiro-miso is white, sweet, and not too salty; inaka-miso is beige-coloured, and a little saltier; and hatcho-miso, rich in protein, is made almost entirely from soya beans, and is the saltiest of all. Available both vacuum-packed and in cans from Japanese supermarkets, it will keep for up to a year if refrigerated.

morteau

A French smoked pork and garlic sausage, about 4cm/1½in in diameter, which is easily distinguished by the wooden sticks used to seal the ends. Available from specialized delicatessens.

noodles

Oil noodles are made with egg, oil and semolina flour, and are the favourite noodles of the Chinese. They are sold fresh in Chinese supermarkets, and require no further cooking other than to be heated through.

Rice noodles/vermicelli are widely available and can be used for numerous South-East Asian dishes. They are sometimes known as rice sticks.

Soba noodles are made with golden buckwheat and are the most popular Japanese noodle. They are thin, flat noodles, often served in soups and broths. They should be cooked in miso, dashi or boiling water, for 2–3 minutes.

nori

A Japanese seaweed, flattened and dried into thin greenish-purple sheets. It is used to wrap sushi, and is also shredded to flavour and decorate soups and salads.

oil

Corn oil is a vegetable oil, often favoured for deep-frying as it has very little flavour and gives a clean taste.

Olive oil, used in cooking throughout the Mediterranean, is pressed from ripe olives and has a strong, distinctive taste. Always use extra virgin olive oil (first pressing), which is the best quality.

Peanut and **sunflower oils** are lighter, and more popular in Eastern cuisine, than olive oils.

Sesame oil is highly aromatic, and is often added in small quantities as a finishing touch to many Chinese dishes.

Truffle oil is made by infusing white or black truffles in olive oil, with white considered the superior version. It is highly aromatic and should be used in small quantities.

Walnut oil is also highly aromatic and should be used sparingly.

oyster sauce

A sauce derived from oysters, water, salt, cornflour and caramel, used in stir-fries and as a seasoning. Beware of imitations, labelled 'Oyster-flavoured Sauce', as these will not give the same depth of flavour.

pak chee laos (ferang)

A type of coriander indigenous to Laos, north-east of Thailand. Unusual in flavour, it is available from good Asian supermarkets.

palmiers

Originating in Paris, these shaped strips of puff pastry are rolled in sugar and cooked in a medium oven until the sugar caramelizes. They are widely available in supermarkets and delicatessens.

pancetta

Smoked Italian belly pork, available in either slices or slabs.

panettone

An Italian bread-like cake, baked around Christmas time, and often filled with dried fruit or covered with chocolate. Available from Italian delicatessens and some supermarkets.

passata

High quality purée of cooked tomatoes, ideal for use in sauces.

Peking duck

Peking duck differs from European ducks in three ways: there is less fat underneath the skin, there is more meat on the breast and, because it is plucked wet rather than dry, it holds a marinade better and hence the skin is crisper when cooked. Peking duck can be bought in Chinese supermarkets fresh or frozen, or even marinated and freshly roasted, or roasted and frozen. Do not use other kinds of duck where Peking duck is specified, as these are quite different. (To roast Peking duck, see page 218.)

pink pickled ginger

Young root ginger, sliced and marinated in rice wine vinegar for several months. Pink pickled ginger is used in Far Eastern cooking, primarily Japanese, as a side dish, seasoning or garnish.

pistachio paste

A concentrated, refined paste made from pistachio nuts, for use in confectionery. This paste is very expensive and is available from specialized delicatessens. Crushed pistachio nuts or pistachio extract can be used as substitutes in most recipes.

rice

There are said to be 7,000 different varieties of rice, generally divided into long-, medium- and short-grain types. The ones most commonly used in the recipes in this book are listed below:

Arborio rice (superfino) is the classic Italian medium-grain rice. It is the best rice to use for risottos as it can absorb a great deal of liquid without becoming too soft.

Black rice is very dark, almost purple, in colour and retains a nuttiness of flavour. It is the unpolished version of sticky rice (see below) and also becomes glutinous when cooked. It needs to be soaked for at least 3 hours before use.

Sticky rice, used in Chinese and Japanese cooking, is a short-grain white rice that becomes glutinous when cooked and is used for both sweet and savoury dishes.

Thai fragrant rice, usually flavoured with jasmine, is slightly aromatic in taste, and is often used for feast dishes in Thai and Vietnamese cooking.

salted duck eggs

Because duck eggs are seasonal, and usually unavailable in winter, salting them is often a good idea – although fresh and salted are not interchangeable by any means. Salted duck eggs can be made at home by soaking in brine for at least four weeks (page 213). They can also be bought in Chinese and Asian supermarkets, but do not confuse them with black salty duck eggs, which are jellied inside and quite unpleasant in taste.

shallots

A vegetable related to onion and garlic, and native to western Asia. The word 'shallot' is derived from 'Ascalon', the city of the Philistines.

Banana shallots, a variation of Thai shallots, are pale purple in colour and are around 10cm/4in long, hence the name.

French shallots are red, about the size of a small onion, with a papery skin and a distinctive flavour. A classic ingredient in many French dishes.

Thai shallots are about 2.5cm/1in in diameter and pale purple in colour. Available in Oriental supermarkets.

shoa sing

A Chinese rice wine used extensively in stir-fries and braised dishes. It is made from fermented water and glutinous rice, and is a rich brown colour. Available from Asian grocers and supermarkets. Dry sherry can be used as a substitute.

shrimp paste

A fermented paste known as *capi* or *kapi*, used to give flavour to Thai curries and soups. Do not confuse with the blocks of paste called *blanchan* used in Malaysian cooking, which are sliced, toasted and crumbled, and which have a quite different taste.

snake beans

Sometimes called yard-long beans, these peppery, elongated beans measure about 1 metre (1 yard) in length, hence the name. Although often found in Asian supermarkets and grocers, they can be replaced with green or French beans and extra black pepper if necessary.

sour green mango

Approximately half the size of the common sweet mango, these vegetables have a firm texture and a sharp end. They can be found in Thai and Asian supermarkets.

soy sauce

The fermented extracted juice of the soya bean. Japanese fermented soy sauce is the type to use as a condiment – other types are more suitable for use in cooking.

Light soy is the most widely used type of soy sauce and is very salty in taste.

Dark soy has a strong flavour and viscous consistency.

Ketchup manis is sweet tasting, with a treacle-like pouring consistency, and is often used as a seasoning for noodles.

sugar

Palm sugar, also known as jaggery, comes in lumps or tablets, and is a deep-flavoured sugar with an intensely sweet taste, rather like molasses. It is often used in the preparation of Thai curries and sauces. Available from specialist stores or Chinese supermarkets.

Rock sugar, a crystallized blend of sugar and honey, has a rich, subtle flavour, and is used in Chinese cooking for sauces or braised dishes. It comes in lumps or slabs, and is available from Chinese supermarkets.

tamarind

Fruit of the tamarind tree growing as pods that vary in size and produce an acidic, reddish-brown pulp, with a very distinctive sour flavour. Tamarind water (page 217) forms an important element in the four Thai principles of cooking – the sour that balances the sweet, salt and hot. Available from Asian grocers, and many mainstream supermarkets, the fruit is bought in tablets of sticky, broken pods, or dried.

Thai sweet basil

Thought to be the original basil, Thai basil – or Asian basil as it is also called – comes from South-East Asia and is used widely in Thai cooking for its strong aniseed flavour and its deep green-purple colour. Also popular in salads combined with mint and coriander.

tofu

High in protein, tofu is the Japanese name for soya bean curd and is used widely in Asian cooking, although not in India. Extremely versatile, it can be eaten raw, boiled or crisply fried, and is particularly popular for patties and savoury cakes.

vanilla

An aromatic flavouring used in sweet sauces, cakes or puddings. Vanilla bean pods are about 15cm/6in long, and are usually sold whole. The simplest way to extract the flavour is to keep pods in a jar of sugar (page 216). Beware of 'vanilla flavouring', which is an imitation of the genuine extraction, and does not compare in flavour.

vinegar

An acidic liquid derived from the oxygenated fermenting of alcohol. Originally made from grapes, and labelled accordingly (e.g. red wine, white wine, Champagne), it is also made from apples (cider), rice and, less commonly, maize and honey. It may also be flavoured by the preserving of berries and fruits such as raspberry or cherry, in a wine vinegar, which gives an added sweetness and colour.

wasabi

Japanese horseradish, used as a condiment in sashimi and sushi, and extremely hot in flavour. It can be bought in root form (in Japanese supermarkets) and grated or as a dried powder, which is then mixed to a paste with water.

USA/Antipodean equivalents

Some of the ingredients and equipment used in this book are known by different names in the USA, Australia and New Zealand. These are listed below.

British	USA/Australia/New Zealand
aubergine	eggplant
bicarbonate of soda	baking soda
celery stick	celery rib
coriander	cilantro/Chinese parsley
courgettes	zucchini
double cream	heavy cream
flat-leaf parsley	Italian parsley/ Continental parsley
frying pan	skillet
greaseproof paper	wax paper
grill	broiler
icing sugar	confectioners' sugar
mangetout	snow pea
muslin	cheesecloth
peppers	capsicums/bell peppers
plain chocolate	semi-sweet chocolate
root ginger	gingerroot
single cream	light cream
spring onions	scallions
sultanas	golden raisins

soups and noodles

For as far back as the records go, soups and noodles have formed an integral part of the diets of virtually every civilization, existing as a staple source of carbohydrate, and providing us with a fascinating insight into the culinary preferences of different races. From the French pot-au-feu to the Italian minestrone, the Russian borscht to the Chinese sharks' fin, the term 'soup' could not be more widely manipulated to reflect the tastes of those who consume it. And similarly, the generic term 'noodle' has been stretched to include basics as diverse as Italian pasta, Japanese bean noodles, German egg noodles and Chinese oil noodles, again, each with as different a taste and texture as is possible to imagine.

Such a heritage of flavours and techniques should not be underestimated, and at Mezzo we strive to reflect this variety in a menu that draws its influence from a number of contrasting sources. Classic dishes have been given a new twist and standard methods adapted to allow for a more modern approach. So choose from Mussels with Lemon Grass and Oil Noodles, Fettuccine with Butternut Squash and Coconut, and Soba Noodles with Raw Tuna and Cucumber Ice, or be seduced by Leek Soup with Crisp Fried Cod or Spinach and Potato Soup: each, their own little taste of history; each that little bit new.

deep-fried rice noodles

spinach and potato soup

A meal on its own, this hearty, warming soup needs little more accompaniment than bread and some good butter. The young spinach leaves are added raw at the end, to give an added freshness. Do not stint on the seasoning: both the potatoes and the spinach need a lot of salt and pepper, and the final addition of lemon juice provides a sharpness that really lifts the dish.

ingredients

serves 4

1 60g/2oz/¼ cup unsalted butter
200g/7oz leeks, sliced into
    1cm/½in rounds
300g/10oz onions, cut lengthwise
    into thin wedges
375g/12oz potatoes, peeled and
    cut into 2.5cm/1in dice
sea salt

2 1 litre/1¾ pints/4 cups chicken or
    vegetable stock, preferably
    homemade (pages 206–7)
475ml/16fl oz/2 cups water
freshly ground black pepper

3 90ml/3fl oz/⅓ cup crème fraîche

4 60g/2oz young leaf spinach,
    washed and drained
1 tbsp lemon juice
2 tbsp olive oil

to serve
chunks of pain de campagne
    (page 163)

method

1 Melt the butter in a large pan over a low heat and sweat the leeks and onions until soft but not coloured, about 10 minutes. Add two-thirds of the potatoes and cook for another 5 minutes. Meanwhile, cook the remaining potatoes in salted boiling water until just soft. Drain and set aside.

2 Add the stock and water to the leeks, onions and potatoes and bring to the boil. Season well and simmer over a low heat for 10 minutes.

3 Remove the soup from the heat and allow to cool slightly, then whizz in a food processor until smooth. Adjust the seasoning and return to the pan. Bring the soup back to the boil, stir in the crème fraîche and cook for a further 2 minutes, then remove from the heat.

4 Mix together the remaining diced potatoes, the spinach, lemon juice and olive oil in a small bowl and season well.

assembly

Arrange the spinach and potato mixture in shallow bowls and pour over the soup. Serve with chunks of pain de campagne.

duck soup with noodles and coriander

If you are roasting the duck yourself, you may never get beyond taking the meat off the bone, as it is so delicious, but persevere and you will quickly discover the advantages of patience and a good stock.

method

1 Preheat the oven to 190°C/375°F/Gas 5. Take the duck meat off the bone (page 218). Halve each duck breast lengthwise, then cut across into chunks about 2.5cm/1in square. Repeat with the thighs and wings. Place the duck on a baking sheet and roast for 15–20 minutes.

2 Bring the water to the boil in a large saucepan. Chop the duck carcass into 4–5 pieces and add to the pan. Place the lemon grass, ginger and lime leaves in a bowl or mortar and crush slightly with the end of a rolling pin or pestle to release the flavours. Add to the pan with the fish sauce and sugar, and simmer over a medium heat for 30 minutes.

3 Pick off the coriander leaves and reserve. Remove the roots from the coriander stalks, crush with the back of a knife, and add to the pan with the star anise. Remove the pan from the heat and leave to infuse for 20 minutes. Taste the stock, adding more fish sauce or sugar as required, then add the dark sesame oil. Strain the stock through a fine sieve or chinois into a second pan.

4 Return the stock to the heat, add the noodles and simmer for 1–2 minutes until warmed through.

assembly

Pour the noodles and stock into a large shallow bowl and place the roasted duck meat on top. Sprinkle with the spring onions and reserved coriander leaves and serve immediately.

ingredients

serves 4

1 *1 Peking duck, home-roasted (page 218) or bought ready-roasted in a Chinese supermarket*

2 *1.5 litres/2½ pints/6¼ cups water*
3 sticks lemon grass, peeled and chopped into 2.5cm/1in pieces
5cm/2in root ginger, peeled and chopped
6 lime leaves, torn
125ml/4fl oz/½ cup fish sauce
30g/1oz/2 tbsp caster sugar

3 *1 bunch coriander leaves, roots included*
2 star anise
½ tsp dark sesame oil

4 *500g/1lb linguine*

to serve
8 spring onions, finely sliced

leek soup with crisp fried cod

Deep-fried cod has long been a favourite because of its soft white flesh and sweet flavour. In this recipe it is teamed with creamy leek and potato soup to create a rich and textured dish.

method

1 Melt the butter in a large pan until browned, then add the leeks, potatoes, celery and ground black pepper. Sweat over a low heat for 5–6 minutes, until the leeks are soft and transparent. Add the stock and simmer for 25–30 minutes, until the potatoes are cooked through. Season well, then transfer to a food processor and process to a fine purée. Return to the pan, check the seasoning, and stir in the crème fraîche.

2 Place the flour in a small bowl and season. Slice the cod into strips 1cm/½in wide, and toss in the flour until coated. Heat the oil in a deep frying pan over a medium heat until shimmering, then deep-fry the cod for 3–4 minutes, or until crispy. Remove from the oil with a slotted spoon and drain on paper towels.

assembly

Warm the soup gently, then pour into bowls and serve with 3 or 4 pieces of crispy cod on top. Finish with a grinding of black pepper.

ingredients

serves 4

1 *60g/2oz/¼ cup butter*
1kg/2lb leeks, trimmed and roughly chopped
500g/1lb potatoes, peeled and diced
1 stick celery, roughly chopped
1 tsp freshly ground black pepper
1 litre/1¾ pints/4 cups vegetable stock, preferably homemade (page 207)
sea salt
90ml/3fl oz/⅓ cup crème fraîche

2 *20g/¾oz/2½ tbsp flour*
200g/7oz cod, bones removed but skin on
600ml/1 pint/2½ cups vegetable oil

to serve
freshly ground black pepper

sweet potato and goat's cheese ravioli in a vegetable broth

The sweetness of the filling adds a new perspective to this traditional Italian dish, though it is the quality of the pasta and stock that is really important.

ingredients

serves 4

1 *375g/12oz sweet potatoes*
375g/12oz goat's cheese, crumbled and any skin removed

2 *500g/1lb pasta dough (page 213)*
flour for dusting
1 egg yolk, lightly beaten

3 *600ml/1 pint/2½ cups vegetable stock, preferably homemade (page 207)*

to serve

½ spring onion, green part only, cut into fine strips lengthwise
freshly ground black pepper

method

1 Preheat the oven to 180°C/350°F/Gas 4. Bake the sweet potatoes for about 40 minutes, or until easily pierced with a skewer. Allow to cool, then peel and roughly mash the potatoes in a bowl with a fork. Stir in the crumbled goat's cheese until thoroughly combined. Place the mixture in a colander and drain off all liquid. Set aside.

2 Roll out the dough to the finest setting on the pasta machine, and halve crosswise. Lay one of the pasta sheets on a floured board, keeping the remaining pasta wrapped so as not to dry out, and mark off into 8 segments. Place a dessertspoonful of the filling in the centre of each segment, brush the pasta with the beaten egg, and lay a second sheet directly on top, pressing down well all round the mixture to remove any air bubbles. Cut into individual rounds 10cm/4in in diameter with a pastry cutter, press firmly to seal the edges and brush off any extra flour.

3 Bring the vegetable stock to the boil in a large pan and gently add the ravioli in batches, allowing them enough room to float to the top and cook evenly. Simmer for 3–4 minutes, then remove from the pan with a slotted spoon.

assembly

Place some of the spring onion in the bottom of each shallow serving bowl and lay 2 ravioli on top. Cover with the stock and season with a grinding of black pepper.

fish soup with lobster ravioli and rouille

This clear fish soup is served with plump lobster ravioli, and makes a delicious alternative to the traditional bisque.

ingredients

serves 4

1 soup
90ml/3fl oz/⅓ cup olive oil
2 medium onions, finely sliced
2 garlic cloves, chopped
5 ripe tomatoes, peeled, deseeded
    and chopped
1 bay leaf
1 bouquet garni
1kg/2lb white fish bones or
    trimmings, or 1 whole whiting
1 pinch saffron
½ red chilli, deseeded and finely sliced
sea salt
freshly ground black pepper
2.5 litres/4 pints/10 cups water

2 ravioli
125g/4oz diced lobster
1 tsp chopped fennel or dill
1 tsp chopped chervil or tarragon
300ml/½ pint/1¼ cups rouille
    (page 208)
500g/1lb pasta dough (page 213)
1 tbsp semolina flour for dusting
1 medium egg, beaten

to serve
chopped chervil or tarragon

method

1 Heat the olive oil in a large pan and sweat the onions over a low heat until soft. Add the garlic, chopped tomatoes, bay leaf and bouquet garni, and simmer for 5–6 minutes until lightly coloured. Add the fish bones, trimmings or whiting, and cook slowly for a further 5 minutes. Add the saffron and chilli and season well. Cover with water and bring to the boil, skimming frequently to remove any scum, and cook for 20 minutes. Strain through a fine conical sieve or muslin, twice if necessary.

2 Mix the lobster and chopped herbs with three-quarters of the rouille to bind the mixture together, and set aside. Roll out the pasta to the second-finest setting on the pasta machine and cut in half crosswise. Lay one half on a work surface dusted with semolina flour. Place a tablespoonful of the lobster mixture at 10cm/4in intervals. Brush the pasta with beaten egg and cover with the second sheet of pasta, pressing firmly around the filling to remove any air and seal the edges. Cut into 10cm/4in squares using a sharp knife or pastry cutter. Bring a large pan of water to the boil, gently add the ravioli and cook for 3–4 minutes. Carefully remove the ravioli with a slotted spoon and drain.

assembly

Reheat the soup. Place the ravioli in individual shallow bowls and pour the soup over the top. Garnish with chopped chervil or tarragon, and the remaining rouille.

fettuccine with cèpes and rosemary

This is a dish to be eaten in early autumn, when the mushrooms are just starting to be gathered, and the nights are drawing in. Rich with the muskiness of fresh and dried cèpes, it calls for full red wine, roaring fires, and a hearty disregard for concerns about waistlines and cholesterol levels.

ingredients

serves 4

1 *90g/3oz/6 tbsp butter*
125g/4oz shallots, finely chopped
3 garlic cloves, sliced
½ tsp freshly ground black pepper

2 *45g/1½oz cèpe powder*
or 45g/1½oz dried cèpes (porcini)
3 sprigs dried rosemary (do not use fresh rosemary as it will make the sauce bitter)

3 *1 tsp white wine vinegar*
475ml/16fl oz/2 cups double cream

4 *1–2 tbsp vegetable oil*
125g/4oz fresh cèpes, sliced 1cm/½in thick
fine sea salt
freshly ground black pepper

5 *375g/12oz dried fettuccine, or 500g/1lb homemade (page 213)*

to serve
freshly ground black pepper

method

1 Melt the butter in a large pan, add the shallots, garlic and black pepper, and sweat over a low heat for 3–4 minutes until soft.

2 Add the cèpe powder or dried cèpes and the leaves from the rosemary sprigs to the shallots and cook over a high heat, stirring constantly, until the shallots turn a pale caramel colour. (Keep scraping the bottom of the pan with a wooden spoon to get up all the flavours.)

3 Add the vinegar and stir well. Pour in the cream, bring to the boil, and simmer for 20 minutes, or until the mixture has darkened in colour and reduced by one-third.

4 Heat a wok or pan until smoking and add half the oil, tilting the pan to coat. Lay the sliced cèpes on a plate and sprinkle with salt and pepper. Place in the pan, with a little more of the oil, and cook until browned on both sides, 2–3 minutes, but do not stir or toss. Remove from the heat and place on a plate to cool, drizzling with the juices from the pan. Add the cèpes and their juices to the cream.

5 Bring a pan of salted water to a rolling boil and add the fettuccine. Cook until *al dente*, or for 3–4 minutes if using fresh pasta, then drain well.

assembly

Return the pasta to the pan, add the cream and cèpes and toss well. Turn out into a large shallow dish, grind black pepper over the top, and serve immediately.

chicken noodles with sake and egg

Sake, a Japanese wine made from white rice, malt and water, gives this dish an edge over other chicken noodle recipes. Traditionally drunk at marriage celebrations to bring prosperity, and offered to the shrines of ancestors as a mark of respect, sake is no ordinary sweet wine, so treat it carefully.

method

1 Heat the wok over a high heat and add the oil. When it is smoking, add the chicken and cook, stirring, for 30 seconds. Add the ginger and the garlic and toss well. Stir-fry for 3–4 minutes until the chicken is almost cooked through and is beginning to brown.

2 Add the spring onions and the noodles to the wok and stir well, tossing to ensure they are evenly heated, 3–4 minutes. Once they are hot, stir in the sake, and then the beaten egg. Immediately remove the wok from the heat and toss. The egg will cook in the heat of the noodles.

3 Stir in the soy sauce, and taste for seasoning, adding a little more if required.

assembly

Transfer the noodles to a large shallow serving bowl and sprinkle with the spring onions. Eat with chopsticks.

ingredients

serves 4

1 *4 tbsp vegetable oil*
4 chicken breasts, skinned and boned, sliced lengthwise about 2cm/¾in thick
5cm/2in root ginger, peeled and very finely sliced (a mandolin is ideal for this)
3 garlic cloves, thinly sliced and cut into strips

2 *125g/4oz spring onions, cut into 7cm/3in pieces and thinly sliced lengthwise*
1kg/2lb oil noodles
250ml/8fl oz/1 cup sake
5 medium eggs, beaten

3 *2 tbsp light soy sauce*

to serve
2 spring onions, sliced diagonally

soba noodles with raw tuna and cucumber ice

This fresh-tasting recipe will do wonders for the most jaded palate. Make sure all the ingredients are well chilled before serving, and always buy the highest grade blue fin sashimi tuna you can find: deep red and glossy, sliced thinly from the centre of the loin.

method

1 Place the chopped cucumber in a food processor and process to a rough paste. Sprinkle with sea salt and set aside for 30 minutes. Drain the cucumber through a fine chinois or sieve over a bowl until all the liquid has drained off. Discard the pulp. Stir the finely diced chilli into the liquid, pour into ice-cube trays or bags and freeze.

2 Combine the dashi, soy sauce, mirin and sugar in a small pan and gently heat until the sugar has dissolved – do not allow to boil. Set aside to cool.

3 Half-fill a large pan with cold water. Bring to the boil and add the noodles, separating them with a spoon or chopsticks as they soften. Bring the water back to the boil, then add 300ml/½ pint/1¼ cups cold water. Return to the boil, and add another 300ml/½ pint/1¼ cups cold water. Finally, bring back to the boil, remove from the heat, and drain the noodles. Allow to cool, then chill. Stir the spring onions into the chilled noodles.

4 Skin the tuna and remove any excess fat. Cut thinly across the grain into 5mm/¼in thick slices.

assembly

Heap the noodles in individual bowls and pour on a little of the dipping sauce. Set a cube of cucumber ice on top and arrange the tuna slices around. Serve with a shallow bowl of dipping sauce and 1 tablespoon wasabi and a few shreds of pink pickled ginger if liked.

ingredients

serves 4

1 *1 cucumber, roughly chopped*
sea salt
½ red chilli, deseeded and finely diced

2 **dipping sauce**
90ml/3fl oz/⅓ cup dashi
2 tsp soy sauce
1 tsp mirin
1 tsp caster sugar

3 *250g/8oz soba noodles*
30g/1oz spring onions, finely chopped

4 *125g/4oz finest grade sashimi tuna*

to serve
2 tbsp grated wasabi, or 2 tbsp wasabi powder, mixed to a paste with a little water
30g/1oz pink pickled ginger

sweet soy noodles with coriander

A meal in itself, this is a wonderfully sensual dish that highlights all that is special about Thai food: soft noodles, sweet sauce, hot chillies and the perfect grassiness of fresh coriander. For authentic noodles, use a pestle and mortar to make the coriander root paste.

ingredients

serves 4

1 *5cm/2in root ginger, peeled and chopped*
8 coriander roots, about 10cm/4in long
5 garlic cloves

2 *4 tbsp sunflower oil*
500g/1lb oil noodles

3 *4 tbsp ketchup manis (sweet soy sauce)*
2 tbsp light soy sauce
60g/2oz sugar snap peas
2 spring onions, thinly sliced diagonally
125g/4oz beansprouts

4 *3 tbsp coriander leaves*
1 red chilli, deseeded and thinly sliced
2 tsp each, deep-fried chillies, shallots and garlic (optional, page 212)

method

1 Place the ginger, coriander roots and garlic in a mortar and pound to a paste. Alternatively, place all the ingredients in a food processor and process well.

2 Place the oil in a wok over a high heat. Stir in 2 tablespoons of the coriander root paste, reserving any remaining paste in the refrigerator for future use, and cook for 30 seconds. Add the noodles and toss, ensuring they are well coated with the paste, for 2–3 minutes.

3 Pour in the ketchup manis and soy sauce and stir well. Cook for a further 3–4 minutes, then add the peas, half the spring onions, and half the beansprouts. Cook for another 1–2 minutes then remove from the heat.

4 In a small bowl, toss the remaining beansprouts and spring onions with the coriander, chilli, and deep-fried chillies, shallots and garlic, if using.

assembly

Tip the noodles into a large serving dish and heap with the coriander mixture.

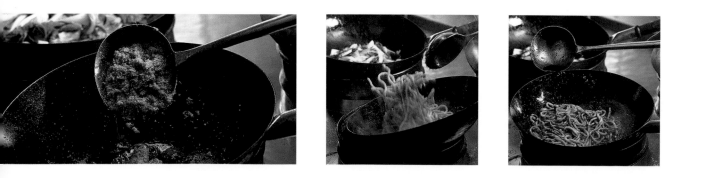

mussels with lemon grass and oil noodles

The warmth of lemon grass and the tang of citrus give this recipe a sophistication that will convert even the most ardent of *moules marinières* fans. Take care to discard any mussels that don't close when tapped.

method

1 Place the tamarind water in a large pan and bring to the boil. Add the stock, lemon grass, lime leaves and sugar and return to the boil. Simmer for 5 minutes, then add the fish sauce, remove from the heat, and set aside.

2 Heat the oil in a large frying pan or wok over a medium heat, and fry the garlic until lightly browned, about 1 minute. Add the mussels and cook over a high heat for 4–5 minutes until they begin to open, tossing constantly to ensure an even heat. Discard any that do not open.

3 Add the stock and the noodles to the pan and bring to the boil, tossing and continuing to cook for 1–2 minutes. Add the chillies and cook for a further 2 minutes, then remove from the heat and season with lemon juice and black pepper to taste.

assembly

Serve in large shallow bowls. Eat with soup spoons, chopsticks, and lots of noise.

ingredients

serves 4

1 *1.25 litres/2 pints/5 cups tamarind water (page 217)*
750ml/1¼ pints/3 cups chicken stock, preferably homemade (page 206)
4 sticks lemon grass, peeled and cut into 7cm/3in pieces
5 lime leaves, torn
60g/2oz cane sugar
60ml/2fl oz/¼ cup fish sauce

2 *2 tbsp vegetable oil*
2 garlic cloves, thinly sliced
1kg/2lb mussels, scrubbed and debearded

3 *500g/1lb oil noodles*
2 red chillies, deseeded and thinly sliced
juice of 2 lemons
freshly ground black pepper

fettuccine with butternut squash and coconut

Big chunks of deep orange butternut squash gently spiced with chillies and curry paste and served over fresh egg pasta create a dish that both looks and tastes fantastic. If you haven't the time to make red chilli paste, buy it ready-made, but given that homemade only takes a 2 minute blitz in the food processor and will keep for up to 3 months in the fridge, it's worth going for the real thing. Always allow the extra 30 minutes for the squash to cool in the sauce, as this allows it to cook gently while keeping all its flavour, something pre-roasting or boiling would immediately diminish.

ingredients

serves 4

1 sauce
  2 tbsp corn oil
  2 tsp chilli paste (page 209)
  900ml/1½ pints/3½ cups coconut
    milk
  150g/5oz creamed coconut
  2 tbsp lime pickle
  30g/1oz palm sugar
  4 tbsp fish sauce
  2 medium butternut squash, about
    1kg/2lb each, peeled, deseeded
    and cut into 2.5cm/1in chunks

2 500g/1lb homemade fettuccine
    (page 213) or 500g/1lb dried

to serve
  125g/4oz fresh beansprouts
  1 red chilli, deseeded and finely
    sliced
  125g/4oz/1½ cups deep-fried
    chillies, shallots and garlic
    (optional, page 212)
  2 tbsp coriander leaves

method

1 Heat a wok or frying pan over a high heat and add the oil. Reduce the heat, add the chilli paste and stir-fry for 30 seconds until fragrant. Add the coconut milk and creamed coconut and bring to the boil. Stir in the lime pickle. Add the palm sugar, crushing it with the back of a spoon until dissolved, and stir in the fish sauce. Taste for seasoning, and add more sugar or fish sauce accordingly. Add the squash to the sauce and return to the boil. Cook for 15 minutes, then remove from the heat, cover and leave to cool for at least 30 minutes. Check that the squash is cooked through, taking care not to stir the sauce as the squash will break up very easily.

2 Cook the pasta in salted boiling water for 3–4 minutes (if using dried, cook until al dente). Drain, and transfer to a large serving bowl.

assembly

Warm the squash sauce and spoon over the pasta. Sprinkle with the beansprouts, chilli, deep-fried chillies, shallots and garlic (if using), and coriander leaves, and serve.

eggs and eggs

Since ancient times, the egg has been associated with a whole host of different myths and rituals, each unique to its own particular civilization. Primitive man saw the egg as a symbol of fertility. The ancient Greeks believed the world was born from a Mother egg; the Romans believed witches scribbled spells on eggshells then flew around in them; seventeenth-century French brides broke eggs as they crossed the thresholds of their new homes, insisting this would bring good fortune. Even today, we continue the centuries-old tradition of decorating eggs for Easter.

Ritual aside, however, the egg is not without its significance. After all, how many different uses are there for an egg? As well as the obvious cooking methods – boiling, poaching, frying, scrambling and baking – eggs are also essential coating agents for breadcrumbing meat and fish; binding agents for ice-creams and sauces; and the prime ingredient in custards, sponges, soufflés and pies. Sauces such as mayonnaise would not exist without the egg.

A glance through the following pages will reveal the infinite versatility of the egg. Choose from Deep-fried Eggs with Sweet Fish Sauce, Steamed Japanese Chicken and Prawn Custard, Truffled Eggs with Potato Salad, or perhaps the simple Poached Egg and Bacon with Lentil Salad – the possibilities are endless. The compliment 'good egg' has never seemed more appropriate.

duck egg

spaghetti carbonara

Spaghetti carbonara is a favourite dish. Perfect for comfort-seeking appetites, it is quick to prepare and makes an excellent meal when your store cupboard is down to the bare essentials.

ingredients

serves 4

1 *sea salt*
1 tbsp olive oil
500g/1lb dried spaghetti

2 *4 tbsp olive oil*
200g/7oz pancetta, or thick sliced smoked streaky bacon, cut into strips 1cm/½in wide
½ tsp freshly ground black pepper

3 *4 medium eggs, lightly beaten*
2 tbsp crème fraîche
2 tbsp finely chopped curly parsley
90g/3oz/½ cup freshly grated Parmesan

to serve

crusty bread, such as pain de campagne (page 163)

method

1 Bring a large pan of salted water to the boil, add the olive oil, and cook the spaghetti until *al dente*. Drain well.

2 Place the olive oil in a large frying pan over a medium heat. Add the pancetta and cook, stirring frequently, for 5–6 minutes, until coloured and slightly crispy. Add the black pepper and cook for another minute. Add the spaghetti and toss with the pancetta and oil until warmed through.

3 Combine the eggs, crème fraîche and parsley and add to the pan. Remove from the heat and stir constantly for 1 minute to allow the heat from the oil and spaghetti to cook the eggs. Stir in three-quarters of the Parmesan.

assembly

Transfer to a large shallow bowl and sprinkle with the remaining Parmesan. Serve with large chunks of crusty bread.

egg raviolo with asparagus and butter sauce

A sophisticated and delicious alternative to asparagus hollandaise, this recipe takes a little preparation, and often some practice – allow for a few broken egg yolks before you reach your required number of ravioli – but it is worth every minute of it. Don't forget to use your thumb to create a cradle for the egg yolks, and do not allow air to become trapped between the layers of pasta, to prevent untimely explosions when cooking.

method

1 Roll out the pasta dough to the finest setting on the pasta machine, and divide crosswise into 2 strips. Beat one of the eggs in a small bowl and use to brush one of the pasta strips. Mark off the strip into 4 segments and press your thumb into the centre of each segment to make a slight hollow. Separate the remaining eggs, one at a time, making sure the yolks remain unbroken, and carefully slide each yolk into one of the pasta hollows. Cover with the second strip of pasta, using your fingers to work out all the air bubbles, then press the edges firmly to seal. Using a 7cm/3in pastry cutter or glass, cut out 4 rounds with the yolks in the centre. Make sure they are well sealed, then transfer to a plate dusted with flour and chill for 30 minutes.

2 Place the wine, vinegar, shallots and thyme in a small pan and simmer gently until the liquid is reduced by two-thirds. Strain through a fine sieve or muslin, and stir in the cream. Return to the heat and bring to the boil, then reduce the heat and add the butter in spoonfuls, whisking until each spoonful is incorporated. Do not allow the sauce to boil. Remove from the heat, stir in the lemon juice and season. Keep warm, preferably in a bain-marie.

3 Blanch the asparagus in boiling water for 5–6 minutes, until tender. Remove with a slotted spoon. Brush with a little melted butter and season.

4 Return the asparagus water to the boil and add the salt and vegetable oil. Gently slide the ravioli into the pan and cook for 1 minute, until the pasta is just cooked. Remove with a slotted spoon and drain.

assembly

Divide the asparagus between 4 plates and place an egg raviolo on top. Drizzle with the butter sauce and serve.

ingredients

serves 4

1 *250g/8oz pasta dough*
  (page 213)
  5 medium eggs
  semolina flour for dusting

2 **butter sauce**
  90ml/3fl oz/⅓ cup white wine
  2 tbsp white wine vinegar
  30g/1oz shallots, finely chopped
  1 sprig thyme
  1 tbsp double cream
  175g/6oz/¾ cup unsalted butter,
    diced
  1 tsp lemon juice
  sea salt
  freshly ground black pepper

3 *20 asparagus spears*
  30g/1oz/2 tbsp unsalted butter,
    melted

4 *pinch of sea salt*
  ½ tbsp vegetable oil

truffled eggs with potato salad

The truffle has long been prized in European cuisine for its distinctive aroma and slightly peppery taste. The two main types of truffle are the white, more flavoursome variety, found only in November and hence sold at huge prices, and the black Périgord truffle. Both are quite inimitable, and a little goes a long way. The recipe below specifies 12 eggs, to make maximum use of the truffle, but only 4 are used in the dish itself. Eat the remaining eggs within 2 weeks and use the rice in a risotto.

ingredients

serves 4
1 truffled eggs
12 medium eggs
1kg/2lb/4½ cups Arborio rice
1 large black truffle, about 60g/2oz

2 potato salad
sea salt
250g/8oz new potatoes, peeled
1 medium egg yolk
freshly ground black pepper
1 tsp Dijon mustard
1 tsp white wine vinegar
90ml/3fl oz/⅓ cup olive oil
1 tbsp chopped chervil
1 tbsp chopped tarragon
1 tbsp capers
1 tbsp small chopped gherkins or
*   cornichons*
1 hard-boiled medium egg, shelled
*   and chopped*

3 *1 tsp vinegar*

method

1 Place a layer of eggs in a large plastic container and sprinkle half the rice on top, placing the truffle in the centre. Make another layer of eggs and rice on top. The rice is used to absorb any moisture from the truffle. Cover and leave in a dark, dry place for 2 days to allow the eggs to absorb the flavour of the truffle.

2 Bring a pan of salted water to the boil and cook the potatoes until tender. Refresh under cold running water and drain well. Cut the potatoes into 2.5cm/1in pieces and set aside. Whisk the egg yolk in a bowl with the salt, pepper and mustard, then add the vinegar. Whisking constantly, slowly pour in the olive oil until it forms a smooth emulsion. If it becomes too thick, add a little more vinegar or warm water. Finish by folding in the herbs, capers, gherkins and chopped hard-boiled egg. Taste and season.

3 Bring a pan of water to the boil, then reduce the heat until it is barely simmering. Add the vinegar. Stir the water to make a whirlpool, then crack 2 of the truffled eggs, one at a time, into the centre. Poach for 4–5 minutes, then remove with a slotted spoon and drain on paper towels. Repeat with another 2 eggs. Cut 4 thin slices from the truffle.

assembly

Gently toss the potatoes in the dressing, warming them first if preferred. Heap the salad on individual plates, and top with a poached egg and a thin slice of truffle to garnish.

fried duck egg and cèpes on toast

Mushrooms on toast is hardly a culinary breakthrough, but in this recipe, using the best new season cèpes and cooking them in the traditional Bordelaise way, there is a twist. Not only does the addition of a fried duck egg add colour, it also gives an incredible flavour, the richness of the yolk blending with the mellow flavour of the cèpes, creating a simple but strikingly different dish that is perfect for lunch or a light supper.

method

1 Heat the oil in a wok or frying pan over a high heat. Add the shallots and garlic, stir for 30 seconds, then add the cèpes. Season well, and add a little extra oil if the pan seems dry. Cook for 5–6 minutes, until the mushrooms are coloured and the juices have begun to run, tossing frequently. Stir in the chopped parsley, cook for another minute, then remove from the heat.

2 Lightly toast each slice of bread, cut in half and place a piece on each plate. Using a slotted spoon, heap the mushrooms on to the toast. Return the pan and the remaining juices to the heat. Add the oil and crack 2 duck eggs into the pan. Cook until the white is firm, then remove from the pan and place on top of the mushrooms. Repeat with the remaining eggs. Drizzle the eggs with the juices from the pan and a squeeze of lemon juice.

Note: the eggs can be cooked in the pan with the mushrooms, if preferred.

assembly

Sprinkle with parsley, and serve immediately.

ingredients

serves 4

1 *4 tbsp vegetable oil*
1 banana shallot or 2 shallots, diced
2 garlic cloves, very finely chopped
250g/8oz cèpes, thickly sliced
sea salt
freshly ground black pepper
2 tbsp roughly chopped flat-leaf parsley

2 *2 thick slices pain de campagne (page 163)*
1 tbsp vegetable oil
4 duck eggs
½ lemon

to serve
1 tbsp chopped flat-leaf parsley

deep-fried eggs with sweet fish sauce

Mention deep-fried eggs and you get the same lip-curling sneer sometimes provoked by such delicacies as jellied eels and pickled walnuts. Such prejudice is quite unjust: deep-fried eggs might sound off-putting, and indeed, they don't look too pretty at first glance, but when you taste them, dipped in the sweet-sourness of the fish sauce, you'll soon be wondering why you got so worked up.

ingredients

serves 4

1 *150g/5oz palm sugar*
4 tbsp fish sauce
2 tbsp tamarind water (page 217)
60g/2oz coriander leaves
60g/2oz/¾ cup deep-fried chillies,
*   shallots and garlic (page 212)*

2 *4 salted duck eggs (page 213)*
250ml/8fl oz/1 cup peanut oil

to serve
coriander leaves

method

1 Gently heat the palm sugar, fish sauce and tamarind water, simmering until the sugar has dissolved (do not allow to boil as this will impair the flavour of the fish sauce). Remove from the heat, allow to cool, then stir in the coriander and the deep-fried chillies, shallots and garlic. Set aside.

2 Bring a small pan of water to the boil and add the eggs, together with a cup of cold water to prevent them cracking. Cook for 8 minutes, then remove and stand under cold running water until cool enough to handle. Shell the eggs. Heat the peanut oil in a medium-sized pan and deep-fry the eggs for 3–4 minutes until golden brown. Remove and drain on paper towels.

assembly

Place the eggs in shallow bowls. Pour over the sauce and sprinkle with coriander leaves to serve. For a more dramatic presentation, slide the eggs on to a kebab skewer.

poached egg and bacon with lentil salad

Some may argue that eggs and bacon need no accompaniment, but once you have tried this version, you'll soon change your mind. Lentils have become increasingly popular and, as this recipe proves, they are infinitely versatile. For perfect poached eggs, place the eggs in the freezer for an hour before cooking.

ingredients

serves 4

1 *250g/8oz/1 cup green or blue*
lentils, soaked in cold water for
2 hours
125ml/4fl oz/½ cup olive oil
475ml/16fl oz/2 cups water
1 garlic clove
2 plum tomatoes, roughly chopped
1 sprig thyme
2 bay leaves
1 tsp freshly ground black pepper
sea salt

2 *1 tsp malt vinegar*
4 medium eggs, chilled in the
freezer for 1 hour

3 *1 tbsp vegetable oil*
4 thick rashers bacon or pancetta,
cut into 1cm/½in strips
2 tsp red wine vinegar

method

1 Preheat the oven to 180°C/350°F/Gas 4. Rinse and drain the lentils and place in a large ovenproof casserole with the olive oil, water, garlic, tomatoes, herbs and seasonings. Bring to the boil, then cover and transfer to the oven. Cook for 25–30 minutes, or until the lentils are cooked through. Taste for seasoning and set aside.

2 Half-fill a frying pan with boiling water over a medium heat, and bring to a gentle simmer. Add the vinegar. Stir the water to make a whirlpool, then crack 2 eggs into the centre of the pan and allow to cook for 1–2 minutes. Remove from the pan with a slotted spoon and drain on paper towels. Repeat with the remaining 2 eggs.

3 Heat the oil in a frying pan and add the bacon. Cook until lightly browned, then remove from the heat. Stir in the vinegar.

assembly

Transfer the lentils to shallow bowls, warming them through first if preferred. Top with a poached egg and bacon strips, then drizzle over the juices from the pan. Season with black pepper and serve.

scrambled eggs with langoustines and crème fraîche

Scrambled eggs with something on the side are pretty much a staple, but in this recipe the eggs are cooked with the langoustines, giving them a much deeper flavour, while crème fraîche adds richness.

method

1 Lightly beat the eggs and stir in the crème fraîche. Season well with salt and pepper. It is important to season the eggs before cooking rather than during, as this enables the flavour of the eggs to come through properly.

2 Melt the butter in a large pan and add the langoustines. Cook for 3–4 minutes over a medium heat until they change colour (if using prawns, cook a little longer). Add the eggs and leave for 30 seconds, then add the herbs and stir well. Cook for 2–3 minutes, then remove from the heat while the eggs are still wet – they will continue to cook while they cool.

3 Toast or grill the bread and place on individual serving plates.

assembly

Heap the eggs and langoustines over the toast, and serve immediately.

ingredients

serves 4

1 *10 medium eggs*
125ml/4fl oz/½ cup crème fraîche
fine sea salt
freshly ground black pepper

2 *150g/5oz/⅔ cup unsalted butter*
250g/8oz raw langoustines or
king prawns, shelled and
deveined (page 82)
30g/1oz basil, chopped
30g/1oz chives, chopped
30g/1oz flat-leaf parsley, chopped
30g/1oz oregano, chopped

3 *4 thick slices pain de campagne*
(page 163)

steamed japanese chicken and prawn custard

Steamed custard, or *chawan-mushi*, occupies a unique place in Japanese cuisine, being the only dish to be eaten with a spoon. It is regarded for the main part as a soup, and its texture is a paradox of firm, set egg custard and a slightly runny inside, as a result of liquid released from the prawns and chicken during cooking. Usually eaten warm, the custard tastes just as good served cold for summer lunches.

method

1 Sprinkle the prawns with a little salt. Drizzle the sake over the chicken. Allow both to stand for 5 minutes, then season the chicken with a little salt and soy sauce. Chop both the prawns and the chicken very finely and divide between 6 ramekins or small rice bowls.

2 Preheat the oven to 180°C/350°F/Gas 4. Beat the eggs until pale and stir in the dashi, salt, soy sauce and the ginger juice. Allow to rest for 5 minutes. Divide the eggs between the 6 ramekins containing the chicken and prawns, filling these no more than three-quarters full. Cover each ramekin with clingfilm and place in a roasting tin. Fill the roasting tin with enough boiling water to come half-way up the side of the ramekins, and cover the whole tin with foil. Place in the oven for 18–20 minutes, until the custard is firm on top but not browned. Be careful not to overcook. Remove the ramekins from the tin and keep warm.

assembly

Serve in the ramekins, topped with a little pink pickled ginger, and with a small bowl of soy sauce for dipping.

ingredients

serves 6
1 *200g/7oz raw prawns, peeled and deveined*
1 tsp sea salt
1 tsp sake
100g/3½oz boned and skinned chicken breast
½ tsp soy sauce

2 custard
6 medium eggs
725ml/1 pint 4fl oz/scant 3 cups dashi
½ tsp sea salt
4 drops light soy sauce
1 tsp ginger juice (page 217)

to serve
30g/1oz pink pickled ginger
light soy sauce for dipping

omelette with asian greens, ginger and garlic

This Thai variation of a classic dish makes a wonderfully quick lunch or light supper. The only effort is in the rolling of the omelette, although this is purely aesthetic, as it tastes just as good folded in half. If cooking for vegetarians, use salt instead of fish sauce.

ingredients

serves 4

1 filling

125ml/4fl oz/½ cup vegetable oil

5cm/2in root ginger, peeled and
    finely sliced

2 cloves garlic, crushed and roughly
    chopped

125g/4oz green bok choi,
    leaves separated

125g/4oz white bok choi,
    leaves separated

200g/7oz choi sum,
    leaves separated

2 tsp sesame oil

½ cucumber, thinly sliced lengthwise,
    ideally using a mandolin

4 tbsp fish sauce

2 omelette

5 medium eggs, lightly beaten

fish sauce to taste

4 tbsp vegetable oil

to serve

fish sauce

method

1 Place the oil in a wok or frying pan over a high heat. Add the ginger and garlic and cook for 1 minute. Add the mixed greens and toss for 3–4 minutes until wilted. Add the sesame oil and cucumber and stir well, cooking for a further 3 minutes. Remove from the heat and stir in the fish sauce. Set aside.

2 Season the beaten eggs with a little fish sauce. Heat a wok or large frying pan over a medium heat and add the oil, tilting the pan to ensure it is evenly coated. Pour in the eggs and roll around until the surface of the pan is covered, using the back of a spoon to spread the thickness of the omelette. Once a skin has formed, allow to cook, still tilting and smoothing, for 3–4 minutes, then lift out of the pan and place on a clean tea towel. At this stage the top of the omelette will still be liquid, but it will continue cooking as it cools. Lay the wilted greens across the omelette and, using the tea towel, lift one edge over the greens. Continue the movement, pulling the omelette over (much like making a Swiss roll), so that the greens are securely enclosed.

assembly

Cut the roll of omelette diagonally into 4 pieces and transfer to individual plates using the flat of the knife. Serve immediately, with extra fish sauce for seasoning.

omelettes stuffed with minced pork

Spiced with garlic, seasoned with fish sauce and wrapped in soft egg, this is the ultimate comfort food. The pork filling can be cooked in advance if preferred.

method

1 Heat a wok or frying pan over a high heat and add the oil. Add the garlic and cook until golden. Reduce the heat, add the onion and sweat until soft. Add the pork and fry for 6–8 minutes, until cooked through. Stir in the beans and fish sauce, tossing well, then add the tomatoes and sugar. Simmer until the sauce begins to thicken, then remove from the heat and stir in the chopped coriander. Season with black pepper.

2 Gently beat the eggs and add the water. Season with the fish sauce. Heat a large frying pan or wok over a high heat and add the oil, tilting the pan to ensure it is evenly coated. When the oil is hot, pour in the egg mixture and roll around until the surface of the pan is coated. Once it has set underneath, cook until the egg is almost cooked through, 3–4 minutes, and remove from the heat. The top of the omelette will still be liquid, but it will continue to cook as it cools. Lay the pork mixture diagonally across the centre of the omelette and fold either side over the filling.

assembly

Tip the folded omelette on to a large serving plate and slice into 4 pieces diagonally. Sprinkle with coriander leaves, and serve.

ingredients

serves 4
1 pork filling
2 tbsp vegetable oil
4 garlic cloves, crushed
1 small onion, finely chopped
250g/8oz minced pork
2 snake/yard-long beans, or
    60g/2oz green beans, chopped
    into 1cm/½in pieces
2 tbsp fish sauce
125g/4oz cherry tomatoes,
    quartered
2 tsp caster sugar
2 tbsp chopped coriander
freshly ground black pepper

2 omelette
6 medium eggs
1 tsp water
1 tbsp fish sauce
3 tbsp vegetable oil

to serve
coriander leaves

shoots and roots

There are two essential rules to the buying of vegetables and leaves: buy in season, and buy the best. Follow these guidelines and you will never go wrong. Of course, you may be tempted by a little taste of summer in the depths of winter – perhaps a tomato salad or spaghetti with fresh pesto – but for all the nostalgic benefits you might reap, there is no comparison with the sheer flavour you would get from tomatoes and basil bought in late summer. One way to temper your culinary influences is to buy organic. Yes, it is a little more expensive and can be harder to get hold of, but these days, virtually every supermarket and grocer offers a strong line in non-forced, non-chemically treated produce, and diets are better for it. Admittedly, organic veg and fruits are often less pretty: big, shiny, bright green cucumbers are the domain of the fertilizer man, as are the bundles of fluorescent orange carrots that, rather than helping you see in the dark, will literally make you glow there. But if you can surmount the aesthetic question your tastebuds will thank you.

From Leeks cooked in Olive Oil with Bayonne Ham, Soused Beetroot Salad with Aïoli and Charred Salmon, to the simplicity of a Tomato Tart with Oregano and Olive Salad, the emphasis has to be on flavour.

sweet potato and black truffle potato

sour yellow curry of vegetables

This curry might more accurately be called sweet-sour: sweet from the pumpkin and sweet potato, and slightly sour from the tamarind water. It can be adapted to suit your own taste (add more curry paste for a hotter flavour) and should be accompanied by plain boiled rice to soak up the juices. If you prefer a creamy curry, increase the amount of coconut milk.

ingredients

serves 4

1 *750ml/1¼ pints/3 cups water*
70ml/2½fl oz/5 tbsp tamarind
  water (page 217)
15g/½oz palm sugar
250g/8oz potatoes, peeled and cut
  into 2.5cm/1in dice
250g/8oz pumpkin or butternut
  squash, peeled, deseeded and
  cut into 2.5cm/1in dice
250g/8oz sweet potatoes, peeled
  and cut into 2.5cm/1in dice
125g/4oz snake/yard-long beans,
  or green beans, cut into
  10cm/4in lengths
100g/3½oz sugar snap peas

2 *4 tbsp vegetable oil*
1 tbsp yellow curry paste
  (page 210)
200g/7oz beansprouts
3 Chinese cabbage leaves,
  shredded
1 red chilli, deseeded and cut into
  thin strips
4 tbsp coconut milk

to serve

2 tbsp coriander leaves
500g/1lb/2¼ cups long-grain rice,
  boiled and drained

method

1 Place the water, tamarind water and palm sugar in a large pan and bring to the boil. Poach the vegetables separately in the liquid until soft, then remove and drain. Do not refresh. (If you are pushed for time, the vegetables can be poached simultaneously. Add in the following sequence, 5 minutes apart, as they cook at different rates: potatoes, sweet potatoes, pumpkin, snake beans and sugar snap peas.)

2 Heat a wok or large pan over a medium heat and add the oil. Fry the curry paste until fragrant, 2–3 minutes, then add the poached vegetables, the beansprouts and cabbage leaves, and the chilli. Cook for 4–5 minutes, stirring, to allow the curry flavours to diffuse, and stir in the coconut milk. Remove from the heat and taste for seasoning.

assembly

Transfer the curry to a large shallow bowl, sprinkle with coriander leaves, and serve with plain boiled rice to absorb some of the heat.

braised vegetables with cous cous and lemon

Inspired by the flavours of traditional Moroccan cooking, this is a gutsy vegetable dish that works well in any setting. Eat it cold on a picnic with vinaigrette and hummus, or warmed through for a quick lunch.

method

1 Place the chickpeas, onion and carrot in a medium pan and cover with water. Bring to the boil, then simmer for about 3 hours, until the chickpeas are soft. Drain, discarding the vegetables, and set aside.

2 Over a low heat, gently toast the cinnamon stick and coriander seeds in a dry shallow pan for 1–2 minutes to bring out the flavour. Place in a mortar or deep bowl with the garlic, cumin, turmeric, ginger, cloves and coriander stalks, and pound into a rough paste. Heat the oil in a large pan, add 2 onions, chopped, and the pounded mixture and sweat over a low heat until soft and fragrant. Add the tomatoes and simmer for 2–3 minutes, then pour in the stock, and bring to the boil. Add the sweet potato, carrots, new potatoes and remaining onions, quartered, and return to the boil. Simmer for 5 minutes, then add the squash. Cook for a further 20–25 minutes until all the vegetables are just soft, then remove from the heat. Stir in the chickpeas and set aside.

3 Place the cous cous in a large bowl with the butter and salt, and pour over the boiling water. Stir well and cover with clingfilm. Leave for 4–5 minutes, then mix in the preserved lemon and taste for seasoning.

assembly

Spoon the cous cous into the bottom of a large bowl and ladle over the chickpeas and vegetables. Sprinkle with the coriander leaves and chilli, and serve.

ingredients

serves 4

1 *250g/8oz/1¼ cups chickpeas, soaked overnight in cold water*
1 medium onion, halved
1 carrot

2 *2.5cm/1in piece cinnamon stick*
½ tsp coriander seeds
4 garlic cloves, finely chopped
1 tsp ground cumin
½ tsp turmeric
2.5cm/1in root ginger, peeled and finely chopped
2 cloves
4 stalks coriander, leaves torn
2 tbsp olive oil
4 medium onions
6 medium tomatoes, diced
2.5 litres/4 pints/10 cups vegetable stock, preferably homemade (page 207)
1 sweet potato, peeled and diced
3 carrots, diced
250g/8oz new potatoes, halved
1 small butternut squash, cubed

3 *250g/8oz/1¼ cups cous cous*
30g/1oz/2 tbsp butter
½ tsp sea salt
475ml/16fl oz/2 cups boiling water
1 preserved lemon (page 212), cut into 1cm/½in squares

to serve
2 tbsp coriander leaves
1 dried red chilli, deseeded and thinly sliced

pappardelle with artichokes and broad beans

Wide ribbons of pasta are combined with globe artichokes, cream sauce and a delicate purée of broad beans to create a delicious supper dish. The herb and olive oil liquid in which the artichokes are cooked should be saved, as it makes a wonderful base for salad dressings, or for cooking Leeks with Bayonne Ham (page 62).

ingredients

serves 4

1 *500g/1lb pasta dough, preferably homemade (page 213) or 500g/1lb dried pappardelle*

2 *500g/1lb baby globe artichokes*
   1 litre/1¾ pints/4 cups water
   ½ lemon
   90ml/3fl oz/⅓ cup white wine vinegar
   600ml/1 pint/2½ cups olive oil
   2 sprigs thyme
   2 bay leaves
   2 garlic cloves
   1 tsp black peppercorns, crushed
   1 tsp coriander seeds, crushed
   1 tsp sea salt

3 *30g/1oz/2 tbsp butter*
   60g/2oz shallots, diced
   250ml/8fl oz/1 cup double cream

4 *500g/1lb broad beans, shelled and inner skin peeled off*
   sea salt
   200ml/7fl oz/scant 1 cup milk
   freshly ground black pepper
   1 tbsp olive oil

method

1 Roll out the pasta on the finest setting of the pasta machine. Allow to dry slightly, then cut into lengths about 2cm/¾in wide. Set aside.

2 Remove the dark outer leaves of the artichokes. Cut off the top 1cm/½in of the leaves, and trim the woodier parts of the stem, reserving all trimmings. As each one is trimmed, place in a pan with the water, lemon half and white wine vinegar. Add the olive oil, thyme, bay leaves, garlic, peppercorns, coriander seeds and salt. Cover with a cartouche (page 220) and bring to the boil. Cook for 10 minutes then remove from the heat and allow the artichokes to cool in the liquid. When cold, remove them with a slotted spoon, reserving the liquid, and slice lengthwise into 8 pieces.

3 Melt the butter in a pan and sweat the shallots over a low heat for 3–4 minutes until soft. Add the artichoke trimmings and cook for 5 minutes. Add 90ml/3fl oz/⅓ cup of the reserved cooking liquid and reduce by half over a medium heat. Add the cream and bring to the boil. Simmer for 2 minutes, then remove from the heat and strain. Taste for seasoning.

4 Cook the beans in salted boiling water for 8–10 minutes until soft. Drain and place in food processor. Bring the milk to the boil to just scald it, then add to the beans, and process to a rough paste. Season well. Place in a bowl and keep warm until ready to serve. Bring a second pan of water to the boil and add the olive oil. Cook the pappardelle for 3–4 minutes until *al dente* (or as directed for dried), and drain well.

assembly

Toss the hot pasta with the sauce and artichokes over a low heat until warmed through. Spoon the broad bean purée into the base of a large serving bowl and heap the pasta on top. Finish with a grinding of black pepper.

artichoke and green bean salad

This earthy, flavourful salad gives new life to the Jerusalem artichoke, which is too often limited to soups or vegetable bakes. A good companion to the more common globe artichoke, the Jerusalem variety is in fact a sunflower tuber, receiving its rather misleading name via a linguistic corruption of the Italian for sunflower, *girasole*. Indigenous to North America, it was brought to Europe in the seventeenth century, but three hundred years on many people are still not quite familiar with it, despite its widespread availability. Give this salad a go and you'll be pleasantly surprised.

method

1 Whisk together the oils, vinegar, lemon juice and sugar, and season well to taste.

2 Trim the stalks of the baby artichokes and remove the tough outer leaves. Cut off the top 1cm/½in of the leaves and trim off the woody parts of the stems. Cut each lengthwise in 4, and rub with half a lemon to prevent discoloration. Peel the Jerusalem artichokes and reserve in a bowl of water with the remaining lemon half. Bring 3 pans of salted water to the boil. Blanch the beans, baby artichokes and the Jerusalem artichokes separately until just cooked, but still crunchy, about 5–6 minutes for the beans, 10–12 minutes for the globe and Jerusalem artichokes, then refresh under cold running water. Slice the Jerusalem artichokes at an angle, 2cm/¾in thick, and place in a bowl with the globe artichokes, beans, parsley and olives. Season well and toss with the dressing.

assembly

Heap the dressed salad on to individual plates, add a grinding of black pepper and serve at room temperature, or chilled if preferred.

ingredients

serves 4

1 *200ml/7fl oz/¾ cup walnut oil*
1 tbsp olive oil
275ml/9fl oz/generous 1 cup red wine vinegar
125ml/4fl oz/½ cup lemon juice
1 tsp caster sugar
sea salt
freshly ground black pepper

2 *200g/7oz baby globe artichokes*
1 lemon
300g/10oz Jerusalem artichokes
250g/8oz green beans, trimmed
30g/1oz flat-leaf parsley
175g/6oz/1 cup pitted black olives

to serve
freshly ground black pepper

leeks cooked in olive oil with bayonne ham

Bayonne ham, from the Basque country of France, is perhaps one of the best known of the Gallic cured hams, and with its sweet, aromatic flavour it is a perfect companion for the leeks in this recipe. The ham is salted in a brine containing red wine, rosemary and olive oil, then wrapped in straw and smoked to produce its inimitable texture and taste.

ingredients

serves 4
1 *475ml/16fl oz/2 cups water*
300ml/½ pint/1¼ cups olive oil
750g/1½lb leeks, dark green leaves
removed, and scored lengthwise
30g/1oz thyme sprigs
1 bay leaf
3 peppercorns, crushed
2 garlic cloves, crushed
6 coriander seeds, crushed
½ tsp sea salt
¼ lemon

to serve
8 slices Bayonne ham, or similar
cured ham such as Parma or
Westphalia

method

1 Place the water and oil in a large pan and bring to the boil. Add the leeks, thyme, bay leaf, peppercorns, garlic, coriander seeds, salt and lemon, and cover with a cartouche (page 220). Simmer for 15 minutes, then remove from the heat and allow the leeks to cool in the liquid.

assembly

Place 2 slices of ham on each plate and heap the cold leeks on top. Drizzle with a little of the cooking liquid and serve.

creamed leek tart

This tart makes perfect picnic fodder. It has a wonderfully delicate flavour, with a crumbly light pastry and a density of filling quiches can only dream of. Do not be tempted to forgo making your own dough in favour of shop-bought: this is a particularly easy recipe that can be done entirely in the food processor if you prefer, so it is well worth overcoming any fears you might have of home baking.

ingredients

serves 8

1 pastry

300g/10oz/2½ cups plain flour, plus
    extra for dusting
150g/5oz/⅔ cup unsalted butter, cut
    into small pieces, plus extra for
    greasing
1 medium egg yolk
4 tbsp iced water

2 leeks

150g/5oz/⅔ cup unsalted butter
1kg/2lb leeks, sliced lengthwise
    and cut into 2.5cm/1in pieces
    sea salt
freshly ground black pepper

3 custard

½ tbsp plain flour
350ml/12fl oz/1½ cups milk
250ml/8fl oz/1 cup double cream
3 medium eggs
4 medium egg yolks

method

1 Place the flour and butter in a mixing bowl and, using a knife, work together until you have a consistency resembling fine breadcrumbs. Alternatively, use a pulse-action food processor. Add the egg yolk and water, and bring together into a ball. Do not knead. Roll the pastry in clingfilm and rest in the refrigerator for at least 1 hour.

2 Heat the butter in a pan and add the leeks, tossing well. Cook over a low heat for 20–25 minutes until soft, then season to taste. Roll out the pastry on a floured board to about 5mm/¼in thick, and gently lay across a 25cm/10in greased loose-bottomed flan tin. Using a small ball made from offcuts, gently press the pastry into the tin and trim, leaving a slight overlap to allow for shrinkage. Line the tin with greaseproof paper and baking beans, then rest in the refrigerator for another 30 minutes. Preheat the oven to 180°C/350°F/Gas 4. Bake blind for 15 minutes, then remove the paper and beans and bake for a further 5 minutes until the pastry is pale golden. Cool on a wire rack. Leave the oven on at the same temperature.

3 Stir the flour into the leeks and cook for another 3–4 minutes before adding the milk and cream. Simmer for 15 minutes to cook out the flour, and season well. Remove from the heat and allow to cool. Add the eggs and egg yolks and mix well. Spoon the mixture into the prepared pastry case and press down well. Bake for 20–25 minutes until puffed and golden. Rest for 15–20 minutes to set.

assembly

Remove the tart from the tin and place on a board or a plate. Serve at room temperature.

beansprout fritters with sweet pork relish

Imagine, if you will, a perfect world where beansprouts taste of something other than bitter water and pork is like popcorn coated in sweet caramel, and you have this recipe, pretty much. Warmed by the bite of soy and fish sauce, and perfectly cut by the tang of shallots, this dish will thrill the most jaded appetite.

method

1 Whisk the egg with the sliced shallots and coriander, and stir in the flour and fish sauce. Leave for 30 minutes to rest. Add the beansprouts to the batter and gather together into a ball with your hands. Divide the mixture into 8 balls and set aside.

2 Preheat the oven to 200°C/400°F/Gas 6. Half-fill a roasting tin with boiling water and balance a wire rack on top. Place the pork on the rack and steam in the oven for 30–40 minutes, until the pork is cooked through and the fat has begun to colour. Allow to cool, then cut the pork into 1cm/½in dice.

3 Heat 250ml/8fl oz/1 cup of the peanut oil in a deep pan and fry the shallots until crisp and golden. Remove the shallots and drain on paper towels. Pour 60ml/2fl oz/¼ cup of the oil into a wok or shallow pan, reserving the remainder, reheat and fry the pork until crisp. Drain most of the oil from the wok, then add the sugar, stirring constantly until it crystallizes and turns to caramel. Mix in the deep-fried shallots and remove from the heat. Carefully add the soy sauce and fish sauce (beware as the pan is likely to spit), and stir well, then leave to cool.

   Reheat the oil in the first pan, adding the remaining oil if necessary, and deep-fry the beansprout fritters until golden, 1–2 minutes. Remove and drain on paper towels.

assembly

Place the fritters in shallow bowls with a spoonful of the sweet pork relish alongside. Scatter with coriander leaves and serve.

ingredients

serves 4
1 1 medium egg
   2 shallots, thinly sliced
   2 tbsp chopped coriander leaves
   30g/1oz/¼ cup plain flour
   1 tsp fish sauce
   125g/4oz beansprouts

2 375g/12oz belly or shoulder pork, boned and skinned

3 350ml/12fl oz/1½ cups peanut oil
   6 shallots, sliced lengthwise
   375g/12oz/1½ cups caster sugar
   2 tsp soy sauce
   2 tbsp fish sauce

to serve
1 tbsp coriander leaves

soused beetroot salad with aïoli and charred salmon

As beetroot is now available both cooked and fresh, not just sour and pickled in jars, there is plenty of scope for using it in a whole variety of combinations. Paired with charred salmon, it provides the perfect earthy contrast to the sweetness of the fish and can be enjoyed both hot and cold.

ingredients

serves 4

1 *90g/3oz/¼ cup redcurrant jelly*
60ml/2fl oz/¼ cup port
60ml/2fl oz/¼ cup malt vinegar
375g/12oz cooked beetroot, cut into
*   2.5cm/1in dice*
sea salt
freshly ground black pepper

2 *2 tbsp red wine vinegar*
90ml/3fl oz/⅓ cup olive oil
2 tsp caster sugar
2 tsp lemon juice

3 *375g/12oz piece of salmon, boned,*
*   with skin on*
vegetable oil, for brushing

to serve
300ml/½ pint/1¼ cups aïoli
*   (page 208)*

method

1 Place the redcurrant jelly, port and malt vinegar in a saucepan and bring to the boil. Simmer for 10–15 minutes, or until the liquid is reduced by half, then add the beetroot, cooking until it is warmed through. Season well and allow to cool. Drain the beetroot, reserving the cooking liquid.

2 Whisk together the vinegar, oil, sugar and lemon juice with 2 tablespoons of the beetroot cooking liquid. Pour over the drained beetroot, toss well and set aside.

3 Preheat the oven to 180°C/350°F/Gas 4 with a baking sheet inside. Preheat a griddle or heavy frying pan. Brush the salmon with a little oil and season well, then place it flesh-side down on the griddle for 4–5 minutes until charred. Remove from the griddle with a fish slice and place skin-side down on the hot baking sheet. Leave in the oven for 4–5 minutes (the centre should still be slightly pink), then remove and allow to cool for 3 minutes. Turn the salmon and peel away the skin. Using a sharp knife, scrape out the grey film (bloodline) beneath the skin, then with a fork gently pull the flesh into large pieces. The salmon will flake apart naturally, and should not be cut.

assembly

Place a small pile of beetroot in the centre of each plate and heap 2 or 3 pieces of salmon on top. Drizzle over a little aïoli and serve.

potato and thyme rösti with onion, rocket and parmesan

If your experience of rösti has been limited to the dried-out, tasteless potato frisbees found in motorway service stations in Switzerland, or its near cousins, the bulletproof discs available in freezer shops, any qualms you might have about this recipe are entirely forgiveable. But you've probably never tried Mezzo's version, piled high with caramelized onions and sweet peppery rocket. Although this glorious creation won't stop a speeding bullet, you might wonder how you ever survived without it.

ingredients

serves 4

1 *6 large roasting potatoes*
sea salt
freshly ground black pepper
2 sprigs thyme, leaves only

2 *1kg/2lb onions, peeled*
125g/4oz/½ cup unsalted butter
2 sprigs thyme, leaves only
2 tbsp red wine vinegar

3 *125ml/4fl oz/½ cup extra virgin*
olive oil
2 tbsp red wine vinegar

4 *½ tbsp olive oil*
knob of unsalted butter

to serve
125g/4oz rocket
60g/2oz Parmesan, shaved
freshly ground black pepper

method

1 Preheat the oven to 220°C/425°F/Gas 7. Roast the potatoes in their skins for about 40 minutes, or until a skewer can be inserted easily. Leave until cool enough to handle, then peel, and grate the potatoes into a large bowl. Season well and mix in the thyme. Shape the potato into a ball (or divide into 4 balls if making individual rösti) and set aside.

2 Slice the onions in half from top to bottom, and then divide each half lengthwise into 4 sections. Heat the butter in a large pan over a low heat until browned, add the onions and sweat until they are translucent. Season well, and stir in the thyme and the vinegar. Cook over a high heat, scraping the bottom of the pan with a wooden spoon to get all the colour, until the onions have turned milky, about 10–15 minutes. Remove from the heat, taste for seasoning and cover.

3 Whisk together the oil and vinegar and set aside.

4 Preheat the grill to medium. Heat the oil and butter in a 25cm/10in frying pan over a medium heat until bubbling. (Use a small omelette pan if making individual rösti.) Add the potato ball and spread it out with the back of a spoon until it fills the pan like a pancake. Reduce the heat and fry for 5–6 minutes until the underside is browned, then place the pan under the grill for about 5 minutes to cook the top.

assembly

Slide the rösti on to a board or plate and heap with the caramelized onions. Toss the rocket in the dressing and pile on top. Finish with shavings of Parmesan and a generous grinding of black pepper.

tomato tart with oregano and olive salad

Using a simple tomato sauce as its starting point, this elegant tart is perfect for early autumn when tomatoes are at their most flavourful. Always allow the tart to cool to room temperature before cutting, but avoid storing in the refrigerator as the filling is liable to lose its texture.

method

1 Heat the oil in a large pan and add the shallots, leek and garlic. Sweat over a low heat until soft, about 3–4 minutes, then add the passata and chopped tomatoes. Simmer for 20 minutes, then add the herbs. Cook for 15 minutes, then purée in a food processor until smooth, and pass through a fine sieve. Season well and allow to cool.

2 Roll out the pastry on a floured board to a circle approximately 5mm/¼in thick. Grease a 23cm/9in loose-bottomed, high-sided flan tin. Press the pastry into the bottom and sides, using a small ball made from pastry offcuts. Trim generously, and line with greaseproof paper and baking beans. Rest in the refrigerator for 30 minutes.

3 Meanwhile, make the oregano and olive salad: mix the olives with the shallots and oregano and pour over the dressing. Leave to marinate for at least 30 minutes.

4 Preheat the oven to 180°C/350°F/Gas 4. Bake the pastry case for 15 minutes. Remove the paper and beans and bake for a further 5 minutes until the pastry is pale golden. Leave to cool on a wire rack. Reduce the oven temperature to 160°C/325°F/Gas 3. Add the cream and beaten eggs to the tomato sauce and taste for seasoning. Place the pastry case on the middle shelf of the oven, and carefully ladle in the sauce. Bake for 40 minutes, until the tomato is just set on top but the centre is still slightly wobbly. Remove from the oven and let the tart sit for 20 minutes, until it is set and easy to cut.

assembly

Serve in wedges, with the olive salad.

ingredients

serves 8

1 filling
2 tbsp olive oil
125g/4oz shallots, finely diced
½ leek, chopped
2 garlic cloves, crushed
250ml/8fl oz/1 cup passata or
    puréed tomatoes
6 tomatoes, preferably roma,
    roughly chopped
1 sprig each flat-leaf parsley, basil,
    rosemary, sage and thyme
¼ tsp celery salt (optional)
2 tsp sea salt
1 tsp freshly ground black pepper

2 *shortcrust pastry (page 216)*
flour for dusting
butter for greasing

3 salad
30g/1oz pitted green olives
30g/1oz shallot, very thinly sliced
1 tbsp oregano
4 tbsp JT's vinaigrette (page 210)

4 *125ml/4fl oz/½ cup double cream*
3 medium eggs, lightly beaten

aubergine and miso pickle with scallop sashimi

Raw scallops may not immediately entice you, but they are surprisingly appealing when combined with sweet aubergine pickle and hot wasabi. Always use the freshest scallops you can find for this recipe.

ingredients

serves 4

1 *1 tbsp peanut oil*
2 medium aubergines, cut into
*   2.5cm/1in dice*

2 *4 tbsp water*
2 tsp caster sugar
2 tbsp red miso

3 *2 spring onions, thinly sliced*
1 tbsp soy sauce

4 *8 large scallops without corals*

to serve
60g/2oz powdered wasabi, mixed
*   to a paste with water, or grated*
*   root wasabi*
90ml/3fl oz/⅓ cup soy sauce

method

1 Heat the peanut oil in a wok, then add the aubergines. Stir-fry over a high heat until lightly browned and soft, about 10 minutes.

2 Heat the water in a small pan and add the sugar and miso. Stir to a paste, then remove from the heat. Do not allow the mixture to cook too long and become treacly: if this happens, add a little cold water and gently cook out.

3 Add the spring onions to the aubergines and stir well over a medium heat. Press down the vegetables with the back of a spoon to release all the juices and cook for 2–3 minutes. Add the miso paste and cook for another 30 seconds. Remove from the heat, allow to cool, then add the soy sauce.

4 Just before serving, slice each raw scallop thinly into 4 rounds about 3mm/⅛in thick.

assembly

Layer the scallops on the left of each plate, and balance with a mound of aubergine on the right. Place 1 teaspoon of wasabi at the top, and a small dipping bowl of soy sauce at the bottom of the plate, and serve.

aubergine ravioli with black butter and capers

This is an innovative way to eat ravioli, which are fried in butter at the last minute to give an unusual texture and density of flavour. The combination of aubergine, capers and sage gives a further twist to this dish.

ingredients

serves 4

1 *2 medium aubergines*
1 garlic clove, thinly sliced
sea salt
freshly ground black pepper
125ml/4fl oz/½ cup olive oil
2 sprigs thyme

2 *1 shallot, finely chopped*
150g/5oz/⅔ cup unsalted butter
125g/4oz button mushrooms,
  finely chopped

3 *500g/1lb pasta dough (page 213)*

4 *1 medium egg, beaten*
juice of 1 lemon
1 tbsp capers
12 sage leaves

method

1 Preheat the oven to 180°C/350°F/Gas 4. Halve the aubergines lengthwise and score the flesh in a criss-cross pattern. Insert the garlic slices into the slits and season well. Drizzle with half the olive oil, lay the thyme sprigs on top, and set on a baking sheet. Roast for 45–50 minutes. Cool slightly, then place in a blender or food processor, adding the thyme leaves, and process to a rough paste.

2 Place the shallot and 30g/1oz/2 tbsp of the butter in a small pan and sweat over a low heat for 3–4 minutes, until soft and transparent. Add the mushrooms and cook until the butter has been absorbed and the mixture is quite dry. Remove from the heat and stir in the aubergine paste. Season well, then place in a fine strainer over a bowl to drain. Allow to cool, then transfer to a bowl and chill in the fridge.

3 Divide the pasta into 2 pieces and roll out each piece to the second-finest setting on the pasta machine. Cover the pasta with clingfilm so that it does not dry out.

4 Brush 1 sheet of pasta with beaten egg and place 8 dessertspoonfuls of the aubergine filling at 7cm/3in intervals. Place the second sheet of pasta on top and press out all the air bubbles with your fingers. Cut out 7cm/3in squares with a pastry cutter or knife and press the edges firmly to seal. Blanch the ravioli in boiling water for 2 minutes, then remove with a slotted spoon. Melt the remaining butter in a large frying pan and add the ravioli. Fry for 1–2 minutes, or until just golden, then turn. Add the lemon juice, capers and sage, and cook for 30 seconds.

assembly

Place 2 ravioli in the centre of each plate and drizzle with the sage, capers and juices from the pan.

potato and celeriac cake with greek salad and feta

This recipe makes light work of an often underestimated vegetable: celeriac. It is a perfect dish for autumn, when tomatoes are a deep ripe red, and cucumbers are at their sharpest. Eat it at room temperature, as the cake will crumble if too hot, and always allow the extra 10 minutes or so for the salad to marinate, in order to bring out its sweetness.

method

1 Peel the celeriac and potatoes and grate into a large mixing bowl. Season well, add the thyme and parsley and stir in the melted butter. Set aside for 1 hour.

2 Mix together the mustard and vinegar until smooth, and slowly whisk in the oils. Season well. Add the chopped cucumber and feta and set aside for 10 minutes.

3 Preheat the grill to medium. Divide the potato mixture into 2 and shape into flattened balls. Place a large frying pan over a high heat with a knob of butter. Add one of the balls and pat out into a round flat cake. Lower the heat and cook for 6–8 minutes until browned underneath. Place the pan under the grill and cook the top for a further 5–6 minutes. Remove and keep warm. Repeat with the second ball. Combine the remaining salad ingredients in a large bowl and pour over the dressing.

assembly

Place the potato and celeriac cakes on a large plate or board and heap with the salad. Grind over a little extra black pepper and serve at room temperature.

ingredients

serves 8

1 1 medium celeriac bulb
2 large roasting potatoes
sea salt
freshly ground black pepper
60g/2oz thyme leaves
60g/2oz flat-leaf parsley, chopped
375g/12 oz/1½ cups unsalted butter, melted

2 1 tbsp Dijon mustard
125ml/4fl oz/½ cup red wine vinegar
2 tsp walnut oil
475ml/16fl oz/2 cups olive oil
250g/8oz cucumber, cut into 2.5cm/1in chunks
175g/6oz feta cheese, cut into 2.5cm/1in cubes

3 2 knobs of unsalted butter
500g/1lb tomatoes, cored and cut into 2.5cm/1in chunks
125g/4oz/¾ cup pitted green olives
60g/2oz coriander, chopped

to serve
freshly ground black pepper

vietnamese vegetable rolls in rice paper

These make a delicious, fresh alternative to fried spring rolls. Made from ground rice and water then dried into sheets, Vietnamese rice paper should not be confused with that used in Western baking to make cake decorations. The wrappers should be softened before use, by dropping into water for 10 seconds.

ingredients

serves 4

1 *60g/2oz vermicelli noodles*
3 Thai shallots, thinly sliced
90g/3oz carrots, cut into julienne strips
90g/3oz daikon radish, cut into julienne strips
90g/3oz spring onions, cut into julienne strips
2 tbsp coriander leaves
2 tbsp Thai basil leaves
90g/3oz choi sum, thinly shredded

2 dressing
3 green chillies, deseeded
2 garlic cloves
1 coriander root
1 Thai shallot, roughly chopped
30g/1oz palm sugar
2 tbsp fresh lime juice
2 tsp fish sauce

3 *8 rice paper wrappers, about 15cm/6in in diameter, available from Asian supermarkets and some delicatessens*

method

1 Soak the noodles in warm water for about 10 minutes until soft, then drain and cut into 2.5cm/1in lengths. Combine the shallots, carrots, daikon radish, spring onions, herbs and choi sum in a bowl, and add the noodles, mixing well.

2 Using a mortar and pestle, crush the chillies, garlic, coriander root and shallot to a rough paste. (Alternatively, combine in a food processor.) Add the palm sugar, pounding until well mixed, and stir in the lime juice and fish sauce, seasoning with a little extra of either to taste.

3 Pour over enough dressing to coat the combined vegetables and noodles, and toss well. Lay the pieces of rice paper on a board, and heap the vegetables across the diameter of the circle. Bring one side of the rice paper over the vegetables and roll up, allowing the vegetables to poke out of either end.

assembly

Place on flat plates and serve with the remaining dressing as a dipping sauce.

grilled mushrooms with polenta and parmesan

With their increasing availability, all types of mushroom, wild and cultivated, are finally being given the prominence they deserve. For this recipe, you should choose the largest flat mushrooms you can find, or use a mixture of field mushrooms. Don't wash the mushrooms, as this makes them watery: simply wipe with a damp cloth or paper towel.

ingredients

serves 4

1 *750g/1½lb/3 cups polenta (page 213)*

2 *8 large flat mushrooms, wiped and stems removed*
freshly ground black pepper
olive oil for grilling

to serve
125g/4oz/1 cup shaved Parmesan
olive oil for drizzling
freshly ground black pepper

method

1 Make the polenta, cover and set aside to keep warm.

2 Preheat the grill to medium. Season the mushrooms well, drizzle with a little olive oil and place, stem-side up, on a grill pan. Grill for 5–6 minutes, until the undersides of the mushrooms have darkened in colour and small beads of water have begun to form around the remains of the stalk.

assembly

Spoon the polenta on to individual plates and top each serving with 2 mushrooms. Lay the Parmesan shavings over the top, drizzle with olive oil and a grinding of black pepper, and serve immediately.

wild mushrooms in a pastry box

This is a good dish for early autumn, when mushrooms are at their finest and there is a plentiful supply. If you have enough time to make it, homemade puff pastry is undeniably superior, but a good quality ready prepared pastry makes a reasonable substitute.

method

1 Roll out the pastry on a lightly floured board to a thickness of 2.5cm/1in, and cut into four 10cm/4in squares. Using a sharp knife, score a border 1cm/½in in from the edge of the pastry, cutting about half-way through, and arrange the squares on a greased baking sheet. Place in the freezer for 30 minutes to chill. Preheat the oven to 200°C/ 400°F/Gas 6.

Remove the squares from the freezer and brush with the beaten egg, wiping off any traces of egg from the baking sheet as this will cause the pastry to stick and prevent it rising evenly. Bake for about 20 minutes, or until golden brown. Leave to cool at room temperature. Lift each square of pastry on to a board with a spatula or fish slice. Using a knife, carefully remove the top halves of the inner squares of pastry created by the scoring, to form 4 shallow boxes. Remove the doughy pastry from the insides of the boxes to create hollows, and trim the edges of the inner squares to provide lids. Cover with foil to keep warm.

2 Preheat a frying pan over a high heat. Place the mushrooms on a plate and season generously. Add the vegetable oil to the pan and then add the mushrooms, allowing them to cook and seal for 1 minute before stir-frying. Repeat this process twice, (sealing, then stir-frying) until the mushrooms are browned. Remove the mushrooms from the pan using a slotted spoon, and reserve. Add half the olive oil to the pan and sauté the garlic and shallots until browned. Take the pan off the heat and add the vinegar, the remaining oil, the mushrooms, and all but 1 tablespoonful of the parsley. Mix well and season. Return to the heat for 30 seconds to warm through.

assembly

Divide the mushrooms between the pastry boxes, drizzle with the juices from the pan, then cover with the pastry lids. Sprinkle with the reserved parsley and serve at once.

ingredients

serves 4

1 *1kg/2lb puff pastry (page 214)*
flour for dusting
butter, for greasing
1 medium egg, beaten

2 *375g/12oz mixed wild mushrooms,*
such as chanterelles, oyster,
shiitake, cèpes or girolles
sea salt
freshly ground black pepper
2 tbsp vegetable oil
60ml/2fl oz/¼ cup olive oil
2 garlic cloves, sliced
60g/2oz shallots, diced
2 tbsp red wine vinegar
30g/1oz flat-leaf parsley, chopped

shells and fishes

Pan-Pacific food, by its very name, evokes the ocean: crabs, lobsters, squid, sea bream, mackerel, red mullet – all are distinctive and vital elements of a style of cooking that depends upon its individual ingredients for its simple, flavourful appeal. Light oils for wok frying or roasting preserve the often-overlooked meatiness of the fish, while herbs such as coriander and Thai basil provide a subtlety that complements rather than attempts to upstage the flavours of the main ingredients. Broths replace cream sauces, again emphasizing the actual rather than the achieved, and store-cupboard staples such as fish sauce and tamarind water ensure a balance of tastes.

And just as there is a secret to cooking seafood, so is there one to buying it. Across the world, waters are rapidly being fished out, causing buyers to look further afield for their catches and resulting in produce that is less fresh than that caught closer to home. Whilst to some extent the occasional dull fish is unavoidable, buying according to season and from a fishmonger you know and return to, is one of the best ways to ensure that your cooking captures the incomparable flavour and quality of a recent catch. Look out for clear glossy eyes and a wet pair of gills, and if you buy 'full round' – the whole fish – as we do at Mezzo, you will always know what you're getting.

scallop shell

preparing crustacea

crab

1 *Place the crab on a firm surface. Grip the back of the shell in one hand, and hold the claws with the other. With a single, strong movement, lever back the shell.*

2 *Using a sharp knife, remove the devil's fingers (the four soft fronds or gills on each side of the body).*

3 *Using a small hammer or oyster knife, crack open the claws and legs.*

lobster

1 *Turn the lobster side-on to your body and, with a sharp knife, pierce the horizontal membrane between the body and the head. Push the knife down firmly, splitting the lobster from head to tail. Remove the flesh.*

2 *Break off the claws and crack them with a small hammer or oyster knife.*

3 *Remove the flesh from the cracked claws.*

langoustine

1 *Holding the body of the langoustine in one hand, take the head between two fingers and twist sharply until it comes away.*

2 *Squash the sides of the body gently between finger and thumb, to crack the shell.*

3 *Slide the meat free of the cracked shell (right).*

1 *Hold the oyster firmly in the palm of your hand (using a cloth to protect your hand is advisable for first-timers). Slide an oyster knife between the top and bottom shell, wiggling it a little to loosen the shells until the knife is 2cm/¾in inside.*

oysters

2 *Twist the knife sharply to pop the lid. Slide the blade along the inside of the top shell and cut the membrane attaching the oyster. Cut beneath the oyster to loosen it.*

3 *Squeeze over a little lemon juice, then serve.*

83

stir-fried king crab with garlic and chilli

Choose a crab that feels heavy for its size, with undamaged claws.

ingredients

serves 2

1 chilli sauce

1 red chilli, deseeded and finely
  chopped
2 garlic cloves, chopped
1cm/½in root ginger, peeled and
  chopped
1½ tbsp rice wine vinegar
1 tsp caster sugar
½ tsp sea salt

2 125ml/4fl oz/½ cup vegetable oil
1 tbsp chilli paste (page 209)
60g/2oz root ginger, peeled and cut
  into julienne strips
1 x 2kg/4lb king crab, boiled, shell
  cracked (page 82) and cleaned
2 tbsp fish sauce
freshly ground black pepper

to serve

1 spring onion, finely sliced

method

1 Blend the chilli, garlic and ginger to a rough paste, using a mortar and pestle or food processor. Add the rice vinegar, sugar and salt, and mix well.

2 Warm the vegetable oil in a wok or large pan over a medium heat and add the chilli paste. Stir-fry for 1–2 minutes until fragrant, then add the ginger and crab. Toss well, reduce the heat, and place a lid or piece of foil over the wok. Allow to steam for 5 minutes, stirring half-way through. Remove the lid and stir in the fish sauce. Season with freshly ground black pepper to taste.

assembly

Transfer the crab and juices to a shallow serving bowl and spoon over the sauce. Scatter the sliced spring onion on top, and serve.

grilled langoustines with lemon and garlic butter

Langoustines, also known as Dublin Bay prawns or scampi, can be bought both fresh and frozen, and are much prized for their delicate, rather sweet, flavour. In this recipe they are griddled to preserve this delicate quality, and served with a simple dressing.

ingredients

serves 4

1 *20 raw langoustines, in the shell,*
   split lengthwise, deveined and
   opened out
2 tsp olive oil
salt
freshly ground black pepper

2 *2 garlic cloves*
90g/3oz/6 tbsp butter
1 lemon
1 tbsp tarragon leaves

to serve
1 lemon, quartered

method

1 Heat a heavy griddle or frying pan over a high heat until just smoking. Roll the langoustines in the olive oil and season well. Place the langoustines flesh-side down on the griddle and cook for 3 minutes, then turn and cook for another 2 minutes. Remove the langoustines from the heat and place in a warmed serving dish.

2 Add the garlic and half the butter to the griddle and allow to melt over a medium heat for 1 minute. Add the remaining butter, and cook for another 2 minutes until it begins to brown. Squeeze over the juice of the lemon and add the tarragon leaves.

assembly

Pour the contents of the griddle pan over the warm langoustines and garnish with wedges of lemon.

scallop and ginger spring rolls

A surprisingly easy but very impressive starter, these Mezzo spring rolls are a wonderfully sweet alternative to the many Chinese versions. They do not keep, however, so deep-fry them just before you're ready to eat.

method

1 To make the dipping sauce, warm the water in a small pan over a low heat and stir in the dashi powder. When it has dissolved, add the soy sauce and bring to the boil. Remove from the heat immediately, and allow to cool.

2 Heat 2 tablespoons of the vegetable oil in a pan, add the fennel and sweat over a low heat until soft. Allow to cool in the pan. Lay the spinach in a colander, pour boiling water over it and drain immediately – this will wilt the spinach, but not cook it. Lay a spring roll wrapper flat on a clean tea towel or cloth, and arrange a thin layer of spinach diagonally across the bottom corner of the wrapper. Cover with a quarter of the fennel, 4 rounds of scallops, 1 tablespoonful pink pickled ginger and a quarter of the coriander leaves. Gently lift the bottom corner of the wrapper and lay it over the filling. Fold the sides over to enclose either end, and then carefully roll up, until the opposite edge folds over. Mix the water and flour to form a paste, and use this to seal the roll. Repeat with the remaining wrappers.

When ready to serve, heat the remaining vegetable oil in a pan over a high heat until smoking, and deep-fry the spring rolls for 4–5 minutes, or until golden. Remove with a slotted spoon and drain on paper towels.

assembly

Slice one of the spring rolls in half on a slight diagonal, and lay the two halves at right angles to one another on a plate. Repeat with the remaining rolls. Accompany with a small bowl of dipping sauce, and serve immediately.

ingredients

serves 4
1 dipping sauce
250ml/8fl oz/1 cup water
1 tsp dashi powder
250ml/8fl oz/1 cup light soy sauce

2 *275ml/9fl oz/1⅛ cups vegetable oil*
1 fennel bulb, finely sliced, ideally on a mandolin
175g/6oz young leaf spinach
4 spring roll wrappers
8 large scallops, without corals, each cut into 2 rounds
4 tbsp pink pickled ginger
60g/2oz coriander leaves
1 tsp water
15g/½oz/1 tbsp plain flour

seared scallops with green mango

A wonderful summer salad, this recipe blends the delicacy of seared scallops with the sourness of lime-dressed green mango.

method

1 Place one-quarter of the mango in a mortar or food processor with the chillies and garlic, and pound or blend to a rough paste. Remove and place in a large bowl. Add the remaining mango, along with the snake beans, peanuts, shrimps and tomatoes, and mix well. Season with the lime juice, palm sugar and fish sauce, and set aside.

2 Heat the oil in a frying pan until very hot. Add the scallops, season well, and fry for 1½ minutes on each side, until browned and just cooked through.

assembly

Heap the salad in the centre of each plate. Place 3 scallops at regular intervals around, scatter with coriander leaves and serve immediately.

ingredients

serves 4

1 *300g/10oz sour green mango, peeled, sliced on a mandolin and cut into julienne strips*
3 green bird's-eye chillies, deseeded
5 garlic cloves
60g/2oz snake/yard-long beans, or green beans, trimmed and cut into 1cm/½in lengths
2 tbsp unsalted roasted peanuts
1 tbsp dried shrimps, toasted under a hot grill for 3–4 minutes
6 cherry tomatoes, cut in half
juice of 2 limes
1 tbsp palm sugar, chopped
1 tbsp fish sauce

3 *1 tbsp vegetable oil*
12 large scallops, with or without corals
sea salt
freshly ground black pepper

to serve
2 tbsp coriander leaves

sliced sour green mango

lobster pot-au-feu with blinis

A version of the more traditional beef pot-au-feu, this recipe uses fresh whole lobster served with a vegetable broth and homemade blinis. Time-consuming to prepare, it is nevertheless well worth the effort. If you are squeamish about killing the live lobster, place it in the freezer first, as this sends it to sleep.

ingredients

serves 2

1 blinis

15g/½oz/1 tbsp fresh yeast or
  2 tsp dried yeast
200ml/7fl oz/scant 1 cup milk,
  at room temperature
150g/5oz/1¼ cups strong white
  bread flour
pinch of salt
4 medium eggs, separated
125g/4oz clarified butter or ghee

2 1 leek, chopped
1 carrot, chopped
1 stick celery, chopped
150ml/¼ pint/⅔ cup chicken stock,
  preferably homemade (page 206)
150ml/¼ pint/⅔ cup fish stock,
  preferably homemade (page 207)
6 new potatoes, chopped
1 daikon or 2 white radishes, chopped
¼ celeriac, chopped
¼ cabbage, chopped
1 sprig marjoram
1 tsp brandy
pinch of saffron

3 1 live lobster, 1.5kg/3lb in weight
1.5 litres/2½ pints/6¼ cups court
  bouillon (page 207)
2 medium eggs

to serve
300ml/½ pint/1¼ cups aïoli
  (page 208)

method

1 Dissolve the yeast in half the milk and add 30g/1oz/¼ cup of the flour. Mix to a rough paste in a bowl, then cover with a warm damp cloth. Leave in a warm place until frothy, approximately 30 minutes. Sift the remaining flour with the salt into a mixing bowl. Make a well in the centre and pour in the egg yolks with the remaining milk. Whisk to form a smooth batter, then stir in the yeast paste. Cover, and leave in a warm place for 30 minutes. Whisk the egg whites until stiff, then fold into the batter. Heat half of the clarified butter in a small frying pan over a medium heat, and pour in half the batter to make a blini about 10cm/4in in diameter. Cook gently until browned on both sides, then remove and keep warm. Repeat with the remaining batter.

2 Place the leek, carrot and celery in a pan with the chicken and fish stocks. Add the potato, daikon, celeriac and cabbage and bring to the boil. Simmer over a medium heat for 15–20 minutes until the vegetables are just cooked, then leave to cool in the pan before stirring in the marjoram, brandy and saffron. Set aside.

3 Kill the lobster by cutting it between the eyes with a cleaver. Place it in the court bouillon and cook over a medium heat for 12–15 minutes. Do not allow to boil. Boil the eggs for 6 minutes in a pan of salted water. Cool under cold running water and shell. Remove the lobster from the court bouillon, divide lengthwise (page 82) and clean. Crack the claws with a small hammer or oyster knife, and place the lobster halves under foil to keep warm. Add 150ml/¼ pint/⅔ cup of the court bouillon to the vegetables and stock and return to the heat.

assembly

Arrange the lobster on a serving plate and pour over the vegetables and stock. Serve with the blinis, each one topped with a whole boiled egg and a drizzle of aïoli.

stir-fried squid with tamarind and crisp shallots

This recipe combines perfectly the four principles of Asian cooking: the sweetness of the squid and choi sum, the sourness of the tamarind, the saltiness of the fish sauce, and the heat of the chillies. Sometimes called 'lucky squid', this dish is reputed to bring great fortune, so choose your dinner companions carefully.

method

1 Slice down the side of the squid body and lie flat on a board. With a sharp knife, score the flesh diagonally in both directions to make a grid pattern, and divide into 4 pieces.

2 Place the palm sugar in a pan with the water and stir over a low heat until dissolved. Increase the heat and bring to the boil, simmering until the liquid is reduced by half, but taking care that the sugar does not caramelize. Remove the pan from the heat and stir in the tamarind water and fish sauce, then return to a low heat and stir, without allowing to boil, until the sauce has blended together. Remove from the heat and leave to cool.

3 Heat a shallow pan or wok over a high heat for 4–5 minutes. Add the oil, and then the squid pieces and tentacles, and cook for about 1 minute, stir-frying all the time, until the squid is lightly browned and curled up. Add the choi sum, stir until it wilts slightly, then add the cucumber. Remove from the heat and toss well. Spoon over a little of the palm sugar sauce.

4 Combine the coriander and the fried chillies, shallots and garlic in a bowl with a little more of the palm sugar sauce and mix well (any sauce left over can be refrigerated and used as a dressing for papaya salad or wok-fried greens).

assembly

Heap the squid, choi sum and cucumber in individual shallow bowls or a single serving dish, and place a spoonful of the coriander mixture on top. Drizzle with the juices from the wok and serve.

ingredients

serves 4

1 500g/1lb squid, or 4 baby squid, cleaned, tentacles reserved

2 475g/15oz palm sugar
1 tbsp water
90ml/3fl oz/⅓ cup tamarind water (page 217)
125ml/4fl oz/½ cup fish sauce

3 4 tbsp vegetable oil
375g/12oz choi sum stalks and flowers, cut into 5cm/2in pieces
1 cucumber, deseeded and thinly sliced diagonally

4 90g/3oz coriander leaves
125g/4oz/1½ cups deep-fried chillies, shallots and garlic (page 212)

crab cakes with tofu

Lighter than many recipes for crab cakes because of the tofu, this is a delicious and healthy twist on an often overworked idea. The coriander and ginger paste is an essential part of this transformation and, combined with the chillies and spring onion, gives the dish a freshness of flavour which means that two crab cakes are never enough. Perfect served with wok-fried greens.

ingredients

serves 2–4

1 *5 coriander roots, roughly chopped*
1cm/½in ginger root, peeled and
roughly chopped
2 spring onions, roughly chopped
1 red chilli, deseeded and chopped
300g/10oz white crab meat
300g/10oz tofu, drained
1 tsp fish sauce, or to taste

2 *200ml/7fl oz/¾ cup vegetable oil*

to serve
125ml/4fl oz/½ cup light soy sauce

method

1 Pound the coriander roots and ginger to a paste using a mortar and pestle, or purée in a food processor. Transfer to a large bowl and stir in the spring onions and chilli. In a separate bowl, mix together the crab meat and tofu. Place the crab mixture in a piece of muslin or in a fine sieve, and squeeze out any moisture until the mixture is quite dry. Stir the crab mixture into the coriander mixture and season with fish sauce to taste.

2 Heat the vegetable oil in a deep pan over a medium heat until shimmering. Shape the crab mixture into 8 small round cakes and deep-fry in the oil until golden. Remove with a slotted spoon and drain on paper towels.

assembly

Serve immediately along with small bowls of light soy sauce for dipping.

deep-fried oysters with parsley and lemon butter

Here is a delicious way to enjoy oysters, which in this recipe are light and golden, and lacking the rather slimy texture that puts many people off eating them raw. The best oysters in Europe are the English Colchesters and Whitstables and the French *marennes vertes* and *marennes blanches*, while America boasts the native Eastern, the Olympia and the imported Japanese oyster, and Australia the Sydney Rock. In cooking, lesser-quality oysters might be used at a push, as particularly delicate flavours are often lost, but remember that the best ingredients will always give the best results.

method

1 Gently beat the butter until pale and soft. Stir in the lemon juice, parsley and salt, and set aside.

2 Pour the oil into a large pan and place over a high heat. Mix the eggs, flour and soy sauce together in a bowl to form a thin batter. Dip the oysters in the batter, then roll in the breadcrumbs. When the oil is shimmering, deep-fry the oysters in batches for 1–2 minutes until golden, then remove with a slotted spoon and drain on paper towels.

assembly

Place the oysters on a large serving dish or platter and serve with the lemon and parsley butter in a bowl on the side.

ingredients

serves 4

1 *125g/4oz/½ cup unsalted butter*
juice of 1 lemon
1 tbsp chopped curly parsley
½ tsp fine sea salt

2 *600ml/1 pint/2½ cups vegetable oil*
2 medium eggs
90g/3oz/¾ cup plain flour
1 tbsp light soy sauce
24 oysters, shucked (page 83)
200g/7oz/3½ cups white
* breadcrumbs*

grilled mackerel with potato cakes and salsa verde

The strong flavour of this sea fish makes it the perfect complement to the mellow potato and sharp salsa verde. The best mackerel are found in early summer, when the fish are a good size and the catches are high. Always eat mackerel when absolutely fresh, with firm flesh, clear eyes and a pearly white belly. Avoid buying in late summer, as this is the spawning season and any you find are likely to be below standard or, quite possibly, straight out of the freezer.

method

1 Cook the potatoes in salted boiling water until just tender, then drain well and mash with a fork or potato masher. Return the pan to the heat and work in the polenta, breaking it down with the back of a spoon until it is combined. Add the butter and olive oil, and season well. Divide the potato mixture into 4 portions and shape into flat cakes.

2 Preheat the grill to medium. Melt the butter in a frying pan over a medium heat and fry the potato cakes until golden, in batches if necessary, about 2 minutes on each side. Remove from the heat and keep warm. Lightly brush the fish with the oil and season. Grill, skin-side up, for 4–5 minutes, until the skin blisters and begins to darken.

assembly

Place the potato cakes in the centre of individual plates, and lay the mackerel fillets over the top. Drizzle with salsa verde and serve with wedges of lemon.

ingredients

serves 4
1 potato cakes
500g/1lb potatoes, peeled and cut into 2.5cm/1in dice
sea salt
2 tbsp ready-made polenta (available from supermarkets and delicatessens) or homemade (page 213)
15g/½oz/1 tbsp unsalted butter
1 tbsp olive oil
freshly ground black pepper

2 *15g/½oz/1 tbsp unsalted butter*
4 x 125g/4oz fillets of mackerel
1 tbsp olive oil

to serve
400ml/14fl oz/1¾ cups salsa verde (page 211) at room temperature
1 lemon, quartered

97

roast skate with miso and ginger salad

With the rise of Pan-Pacific cooking, this much-overlooked fish has been given a new lease of life. Here it is served with spinach wilted in dashi, the traditional Japanese fish stock made from dried bonito flakes and konbu (dried seaweed), and enlivened by a ginger salad.

ingredients

serves 4

1 60g/2oz root ginger, peeled and cut into julienne strips
1 tsp caster sugar
1 tsp soy sauce
4 tsp dashi
2 tsp pink pickled ginger
60g/2oz spring onions, finely chopped

2 1.5 litres/2½ pints/6¼ cups dashi
125ml/4fl oz/½ cup red miso
60g/2oz tofu
175g/6oz spring onions, finely chopped
250g/8oz spinach
75g/2½oz pink pickled ginger

3 4 wings of skate, about 200g/7oz each
sea salt
freshly ground black pepper
2–3 tbsp vegetable oil

method

1 Blanch the ginger strips in boiling water for 1 minute, then drain. In a small pan, mix the sugar with the soy sauce and dashi and place over a medium heat. Add 2 teaspoonfuls of the blanched ginger, stir and remove from the heat. Allow to cool, then add the pink pickled ginger and spring onions, and set aside.

2 Heat the dashi in a large pan and stir in the red miso and tofu. Mix in 125g/4oz of the spring onions, and bring to the boil. Place the spinach in a large bowl and pour over the boiling dashi mixture. Stir well and leave to cool. In a separate bowl, mix together the pickled ginger, the remaining blanched ginger and the remaining spring onions, and set aside.

3 Preheat the oven to 400°C/200°F/Gas 6. Trim the ruffled edges of the skate wings with scissors to improve their shape, and season well. Rub the fish with the oil. Heat a frying pan or griddle until smoking, brush with a little oil, and sear the fish for 1–2 minutes on each side, in batches if necessary. Transfer the fish to a baking sheet. Cook in the oven for 4–5 minutes until the fish is cooked through and firm to the touch. Meanwhile, transfer the spinach and dashi to a large pan and reheat.

assembly

Remove the spinach with a slotted spoon and place in shallow bowls. Pour over a little of the soy and sugar dressing, and place a skate wing on top. Garnish with the mixed gingers and spring onion, and serve.

crisp-skinned cod with champ

Because cod is such a meaty fish, it works well with substantial partners such as mashed potato champ. Ask the fishmonger to cut the fillets across the width of the fish, rather than offering you a straggly tail end, and always plump the flesh together before cooking to give a high, solid shape and ensure the juices are retained.

ingredients

serves 4

1 *1kg/2lb potatoes, peeled*
sea salt
90g/3oz/6 tbsp unsalted butter
freshly ground black pepper
125ml/4fl oz/½ cup double cream
6 spring onions, roughly chopped,
*   green and white parts separate*

2 *4 x 150g/5oz fillets of cod*
vegetable oil for brushing

to serve
1 lemon, quartered
freshly ground black pepper

method

1 Place the potatoes in a large pan and cover with cold salted water. Bring to the boil and simmer for 20–25 minutes until just tender. Drain well and mash with a fork or potato masher. Mix in two-thirds of the butter and season to taste. Bring the cream to the boil in a medium pan with the remaining butter. Stir in the white spring onions and the mashed potato and stir vigorously over a medium heat for 4–5 minutes until smooth. Remove from the heat, mix in the green spring onions and season to taste. Cover and keep warm.

2 Preheat the oven to 200°C/400°F/Gas 6. Brush the cod fillets with a little oil and season. Heat a griddle or frying pan over a high heat and sear the cod, skin-side down, for 2–3 minutes. Transfer the griddle or pan to the oven and roast for a further 4–6 minutes, or until the fish is just cooked through and firm to the touch.

assembly

Spoon a mound of champ into 4 shallow bowls and place a cod fillet on top. Serve with lemon quarters and a grinding of black pepper.

roast hake in bacon with spring vegetable broth

Fish and bacon is a classic combination which works particularly well in the case of hake, the saltiness of the bacon adding a bite to this rather delicate fish. Cook hake the day you buy it as it loses freshness very quickly.

method

1 Lay 6 slices of the pancetta side by side on a work surface. Place a hake fillet on top, squeezing it to create a rounder shape. Season, then roll up in the pancetta, pulling each slice firmly around the fish. Wrap tightly in greased foil and secure the ends with a twist. Repeat with the remaining fish and chill for at least 2 hours.

2 Bring half the fish stock to the boil in a large pan and add the vegetables in the following sequence, each 2–3 minutes apart: carrot, celery, broad beans, leek, peas. Cook for a further 2 minutes, then remove with a slotted spoon and place in the remaining cold fish stock to cool. Set aside.

3 Melt the butter in a pan and gently sweat the shallots over a low heat until soft. Place with the herbs in a food processor. Strain the second batch of fish stock, reserving the vegetables, and pour into the food processor with the first batch. Process until well combined, then pour into a deep pan.

4 Preheat the oven to 240°C/475°F/Gas 9. Heat the oil in a large frying pan. Cook the hake rolls, in foil, for 2–3 minutes, turning several times, then place on a baking sheet in the oven for 6–8 minutes. Remove from the oven and rest for 2–3 minutes. Remove the foil and cook for another 1–2 minutes, or until the bacon is crispy and the fish is firm to the touch.

5 Return the stock to the boil and add the vegetables and the cabbage. Simmer for 2–3 minutes, then add the parsley. Season with salt, pepper and a squeeze of lemon.

assembly

Place a piece of hake in each bowl and spoon around the vegetables and herb stock. Sprinkle with salt and pepper.

ingredients

serves 4

1 *24 thin slices pancetta*
4 fillets of hake, about 175g/6oz each, skin removed
sea salt
freshly ground black pepper
butter or oil for greasing

2 *600ml/1 pint/2½ cups fish stock, preferably homemade (page 207)*
1 carrot, cut into 1cm/½in lengths
1 stick celery, cut into 1cm/½in lengths
125g/4oz broad beans, shelled and skinned (optional)
1 leek, cut into 1cm/½in lengths
250g/8oz peas in the pod, shelled, or 60g/2oz frozen petits pois

3 *60g/2oz/¼ cup butter*
125g/4oz shallots, thinly sliced
15g/½ oz basil leaves
15g/½ oz chervil leaves

4 *1 tbsp corn oil*

5 *15g/½oz savoy cabbage, cut into 1cm/½in squares*
1 tbsp flat-leaf parsley leaves
squeeze of lemon juice

to serve
sea salt
freshly ground black pepper

red mullet with potatoes and black olives

Red mullet is a perfect companion for stronger, saltier ingredients such as olives or anchovies, its bright rosy colour ensuring it can hold its own on any plate. In this recipe, black olives are simmered in a garlicky mixture of onions, tomatoes and potatoes, so make sure you have plenty of fresh bread on hand to mop up the juices.

ingredients

serves 4

1 *300ml/½ pint/1¼ cups olive oil*
400g/13oz new potatoes, scrubbed and cut into 2.5cm/1in chunks
200g/7oz tomatoes, cut into 2cm/¾in chunks
200g/7oz small onions, halved top to bottom
2 garlic cloves, finely chopped
2 sprigs thyme
2 sprigs sage
sea salt
freshly ground black pepper
60g/2oz/½ cup pitted black olives
60g/2oz flat-leaf parsley, stems removed

2 *8 fillets of red mullet, skinned and pin-boned (page 221)*
vegetable oil to drizzle

method

1 Preheat the oven to 190°C/375°F/Gas 5. Warm the olive oil in a heavy casserole over a medium heat. Add the potatoes, tomatoes, onions, garlic, thyme and sage, and bring to the boil. Season well and simmer for 8–10 minutes, then cover and cook in the oven for at least an hour, or until the potatoes are cooked through (do not stir as this will break up the vegetables). Allow to cool slightly, then add the olives and parsley.

2 Heat a griddle or frying pan over a high heat until smoking. Season the fillets and drizzle with a little oil. Place the fillets skin-side down on the griddle for 30 seconds, then flip them over and cook for a further 30 seconds.

assembly

Spoon the vegetable mixture into shallow bowls and criss-cross 2 fillets of mullet on top of each one.

grilled sea bream with aubergine and anchovies

The sea bream is a richly flavoured saltwater fish that combines particularly well with such strong flavours as Parmesan and anchovy. Always check for freshness by choosing fish with glossy eyes and firm flesh.

ingredients

serves 4

1 *2 aubergines, sliced 1cm/½in thick*
lengthwise
sea salt
90ml/3fl oz/⅓ cup olive oil
1 garlic clove, sliced in half
30g/1oz basil, chopped
250g/8oz/2 cups freshly grated
Parmesan
1 tbsp freshly ground black pepper

2 *100g/3½oz canned anchovies*
4 garlic cloves
½ tbsp olive oil
freshly ground black pepper

3 *8 fillets of bream, 90–125g/3–4oz*
each
vegetable oil for brushing

to serve
60g/2oz rocket

method

1 Preheat the oven to 180°C/350°F/Gas 4. Lightly salt the slices of aubergine and set aside in a colander for 30 minutes to extract the bitter juices. Wipe off the salt with paper towels. Oil a 15cm/6in square cake tin with a little olive oil, and rub with half a clove of garlic. Oil the slices of aubergine and rub with garlic. Place a layer of aubergine in the tin and sprinkle with a thin layer of basil, Parmesan and black pepper. Repeat crosswise, so that the second layer is at right angles to the first, until there are 4 layers. Bake for 2–2¼ hours, or until the aubergine is cooked through and easily pierced with a skewer or fork.

2 Place the anchovies and garlic in a blender or food processor and process to a rough paste. Slowly add the olive oil as the machine is running, until the sauce is smooth. Season with black pepper.

3 Keep the oven at the same temperature. Heat a griddle or frying pan until smoking. Season the fillets of bream with black pepper and brush with a little oil. Cook, skin-side down, for 1–2 minutes until the skin is coloured, then place the griddle in the oven, covered with foil, for 10 minutes, until the fish is just cooked through. Meanwhile, warm the anchovy sauce in a small pan over a low heat.

assembly

Cut the aubergine cake into 4 squares and place in the centre of individual plates. Lay 2 fillets of bream on top, and drizzle with a little anchovy sauce. Heap some rocket on top of the fish and serve.

salmon in saffron broth with tomatoes

Essentially, this is a recipe for late summer, when tomatoes are at their best and the wild salmon season is about to end, but if you buy your ingredients carefully it will taste fantastic at any time of year. The secret is in the tomatoes: choose them by smell rather than sight, to find the deep fruitiness of unforced tomatoes.

method

1 Preheat the oven to 200°C/400°F/Gas 6. Heat the butter in a casserole over a medium heat until bubbling, then add the tomatoes and tarragon sprigs. Cook for 8–10 minutes until the tomatoes begin to caramelize, and add the salt. Toast the saffron in a dry, shallow pan for 1–2 minutes and add to the tomatoes. Stir in the vinegar, then add the water and wine and bring to the boil. Simmer for 3–4 minutes, then cover and bake in the oven for 30–40 minutes.

2 Lay the salmon on a board and squeeze the sides and ends towards the centre to give a solid, high shape. Trim each end, then cut crosswise into 4 pieces about 7cm/3in wide. Leave in the refrigerator until ready to cook.

3 Remove the tomatoes from the oven and crush with the back of a spoon to release the juices. Strain off the broth through a conical sieve into a shallow pan, return the tomatoes and tarragon to the casserole and set aside. Place the salmon skin-side down in the broth and cover with a cartouche (page 220). Cook for 5–6 minutes, then turn over. Remove the skin and the grey flesh just under the skin by scraping with a sharp knife, and cook for a further 5 minutes, still under the cartouche, until the outside is pale pink but the inside is raw. Remove from the heat and lift out the salmon. Pour the broth back over the crushed tomatoes and reheat. Stir in the coriander leaves.

assembly

Spoon the tomatoes and broth into shallow bowls and lay the fillets of salmon on top.

ingredients

serves 4

1 *125g/4oz/½ cup butter*
1kg/2lb roma tomatoes, or any good tomato in season
2 sprigs tarragon
1 tsp sea salt
pinch of saffron
4 tbsp white wine vinegar
250ml/8fl oz/1 cup water
250ml/8fl oz/1 cup white wine

2 *1 fillet of salmon about 1kg/2lb, pin-boned (page 221), or 4 x 175g/6oz fillets, chilled*

3 *1 tbsp coriander leaves*

beasts and birds

Meat, perhaps more than any other food, has always been treated with ceremony. Often this has been due to a particular regard for the animal or fowl itself but sometimes it has had more to do with the faiths and fashions of the predator. In ancient Thailand, for example, a cow would be divided up according to the status of the eater: the liver, considered the superior organ, would always be given to the king, with the lesser cuts handed out to his immediate subjects, and so on down the social scale. Recipes illustrate a similar hierarchy, calves' liver generally receiving considerably better treatment than other parts of the anatomy, and not without reason: after all, who would want to impress the person who got the tail?

In this chapter such prejudices live on. The following recipes call unashamedly for good cuts of meat, and healthy well-reared birds, with not a dish involving the tails in sight. And just as there is propriety in the serving, so too is there in the basic preparations: never season meat until just before cooking, as salt draws out the juices and will cause it to become dry; always oil the meat itself, rather than the pan, as this will inhibit burning; never butcher meat warm, as it will lose its shape and firmness; and wherever possible, sear meat in a hot pan before roasting, as this seals in the juices and results in the best flavour.

griddled chicken with sea-spiced aubergine

This is an easy-to-make dish that looks and tastes deceptively elaborate. Do not be tempted to season the chicken before cooking: the aubergine has more than enough flavour for both.

method

1 Place the aubergine strips in a wok or frying pan and cover with cold water. Bring to the boil, then remove from the heat, drain, and allow to cool. Dry the wok, place over a high heat with the vegetable oil and add the cooled aubergine. Make sure it is evenly seared, but avoid too much stirring as this will make it mushy. Cook for 5–6 minutes until the aubergine is well browned, then stir in three-quarters of the spring onions and two-thirds of the chillies. Drain off most of the oil, then return to the heat and stir in the oyster sauce and fish sauce. Cook for 2 minutes and set aside.

2 Preheat the oven to 180°C/350°F/Gas 4. In a small bowl mix together the remaining chillies and spring onions with the coriander leaves and the ginger. Gently peel back the skin from the chicken breasts and spread the herb mixture evenly over the flesh. Pull the skin back over the flesh and brush with a little oil. Heat a griddle or frying pan until smoking and cook the breasts, skin-side down, for 2 minutes. Turn and sear the other side for 2 minutes, then remove from the pan and place on a baking sheet. Roast in the oven for 10–15 minutes, until just cooked through, then remove from the oven and allow to rest.

assembly

Place a mound of aubergine on each plate and a piece of chicken on top. Heap with deep-fried spring onions.

ingredients

serves 4

1 2 medium aubergines, cut lengthwise into 1cm/½in strips
125ml/4fl oz/½ cup vegetable oil
4 spring onions, thinly sliced diagonally
3 red chillies, deseeded and thinly sliced
4 tbsp Thai oyster sauce
1 tbsp fish sauce

2 2 tbsp coriander leaves
2.5cm/1in root ginger, peeled and cut into fine julienne strips
4 chicken breasts, skin on
vegetable oil for brushing

to serve
30g/1oz/1 cup deep-fried spring onions (page 212)

roast duck with red curry

Duck with red curry is an inspired combination of flavours. This is an example of a dish with several possible shortcuts, but which will always taste better prepared the long way round: that is, with homemade curry paste and home-roasted duck.

ingredients

serves 4

1   *1 Peking duck, home-roasted (page 218), or bought ready-roasted from a Chinese supermarket*

2   *500g/1lb coconut cream (page 10)*
    2 tbsp vegetable oil
    1 tbsp red curry paste (page 210)
    2 tbsp fish sauce
    60g/2oz palm sugar
    2 x 400ml/14fl oz cans coconut milk, or homemade (page 10)
    10 lime leaves
    60g/2oz coriander leaves
    60g/2oz Thai basil leaves

to serve

1 tbsp coriander leaves
500g/1lb/2¼ cups white rice, steamed or boiled

method

1   Preheat the oven to 190°C/375°F/Gas 5. Take the duck meat off the bone (page 218). Halve each duck breast lengthwise, then cut across into chunks about 2.5cm/1in square. Repeat with the thighs and wings. Place the duck pieces on a baking sheet and roast for 8–10 minutes.

2   Scrape the fat (the gluey liquid at the top of the packet) from the coconut cream and heat it in a large wok or frying pan over a low heat with the oil. Add the red curry paste and fry until fragrant, 30 seconds. Add the remaining coconut cream and stir well until mixed. Add the fish sauce and palm sugar, breaking it down with the back of a spoon until combined, and then the coconut milk and lime leaves. Bring to the boil, then lower the heat and simmer for 18–20 minutes. Add the coriander and basil leaves.

assembly

Place the duck pieces in the bottom of a shallow serving bowl and cover with the curry sauce. Sprinkle with coriander leaves and serve with bowls of rice.

confit of duck with white beans and sage

Confit of duck was first developed in south-west France as an economical means of storing meat in a climate where it would otherwise deteriorate quickly. It is a process that can also be applied successfully to goose and pork. Prepare the confit at least a week ahead to give the flavours a chance to develop.

ingredients

serves 4

1 *4 duck legs, 250–300g/8–10oz each*
60g/2oz sea salt
1 tsp freshly ground black pepper
2 garlic cloves, crushed
4 sprigs thyme

2 *1kg/2lb goose or duck fat*

3 *375g/12oz/1¾ cups dried white*
haricot beans
1 carrot, chopped
1 medium onion, chopped
4 tomatoes, chopped
1 bouquet garni
2 sprigs flat-leaf parsley
2 sprigs thyme
2 sprigs sage
4 tbsp olive oil
125g/4oz pancetta, cut into
thin lardons

to serve
sage leaves

method

1 Season the duck legs and place them in a roasting tin. Dot with the garlic and thyme, and leave overnight in the refrigerator (do not leave longer than 24 hours or the duck will absorb too much salt and become dry).

2 Melt the goose fat in a large pan. Wipe the salt from the duck with paper towels and place the duck in the melted fat. Slowly bring to the boil, then lower the heat and cook gently for 2½–3 hours. Test with a skewer to check that the meat is tender, then remove from the heat and allow to cool in the fat. When cold, remove the duck and set aside. Spoon the fat into a large bowl, refrigerate until it sets, then turn out on to a plate and skim off the jelly at the base (this can be used in gravies or sauces). Return the fat to the pan and bring to the boil, then allow to cool. Quarter-fill a large jar or plastic box with fat and lay the duck legs inside. Cover with the remaining fat and store in the refrigerator for at least 4–5 days before serving.

3 The day before serving, soak the beans in cold water and leave overnight. The next day, rinse and cover with cold water. Add the vegetables, herbs, olive oil and pancetta, and bring to the boil. Simmer for 1 hour, or until the beans are soft. Drain off the excess liquid, discarding the herb sprigs and bouquet garni. The beans should have the texture of a thick soup. When ready to serve, preheat the oven to 180°/350°F/Gas 4. Remove the duck legs from the fat. Heat an ovenproof frying pan until hot, add the duck legs skin-side down and cook for 4 minutes. Turn the legs and place the pan in the oven for approximately 20 minutes.

assembly

Pour the beans into shallow bowls and place a piece of duck on top. Garnish with sage leaves.

crisp fried quail with young carrot salad and gremolata

A member of the partridge family, the quail is prized for its delicate flavour. Although many are now farmed, and hence available all year round, they are still considered to be at their best in the autumn. Quail are small birds, and as a general rule you should allow two per person.

ingredients

serves 4

1 *500g/1lb baby carrots*
90ml/3fl oz/⅓ cup olive oil
125ml/4fl oz/½ cup water
juice of ½ lemon
1 garlic clove, crushed
sea salt
freshly ground black pepper

2 gremolata
zest of 1 lemon, finely grated
1 garlic clove, finely chopped
90g/3oz flat-leaf parsley, finely
  chopped
¼ tsp sea salt
pinch of freshly ground black pepper

3 *1 litre/1¾ pints/4 cups vegetable oil*
30g/1oz/¼ cup rice flour
½ tsp five-spice powder
1 spring onion, very finely diced
8 quail, spatchcocked (page 221)

method

1 Place the carrots, oil, water, lemon juice, garlic and seasoning in a heavy pan and bring to the boil over a high heat. Cover and leave to simmer for 3 minutes, then remove from the heat. The carrots will continue to cook as they cool. Drain the carrots when cool, reserving the cooking liquid, and set aside.

2 Mix together the grated lemon zest, garlic, parsley, salt and pepper, and set aside.

3 Place the oil in a large heavy pan or deep-fat fryer over a medium heat. Mix together the rice flour, five-spice powder and spring onion until well combined. Toss the quail in the flour until they are evenly coated, then drop them into the hot oil, 4 at a time. Cook for about 10 minutes, until they are crispy. Remove from the oil with a slotted spoon, drain on paper towels, and keep warm in the oven while the second batch of quail is cooked.

assembly

Spoon the carrots into individual bowls or plates, dress with a little of the reserved carrot liquor, and place 2 quail on top of each serving. Sprinkle with gremolata, and serve at once.

poached chicken and coconut salad on banana leaf

Chicken thigh meat is used in this recipe in preference to breast because it has more flavour. It is poached in coconut milk and palm sugar to ensure a sweetness and texture that would be lost with drier methods of cooking. The vegetables should be sliced as thinly as possible, ideally using a Japanese mandolin.

ingredients

serves 4

1 *1 x 400ml/14fl oz tin coconut milk, or homemade (page 10)*
60ml/2fl oz/¼ cup fish sauce
60g/2oz palm sugar
875g/1¾lb chicken thighs, boned

2 *2 red Thai shallots, thinly sliced*
½ red pepper, deseeded and cut into julienne strips
2 small red chillies, deseeded and very finely sliced
¼ cucumber, deseeded and cut into julienne strips
4 lime leaves, cut into julienne strips
30g/1oz coriander leaves
2 tsp unsalted roasted peanuts

3 *2 tsp vegetable oil*
1 banana leaf, cut into 4 x 20cm/8in squares

method

1 Place the coconut milk, fish sauce and palm sugar in a large pan and warm gently, breaking up the sugar with the back of a spoon until it is dissolved. Add the chicken meat and bring to the boil. Poach for 4–5 minutes, then remove from the heat. Allow to cool in the pan – the chicken will continue cooking – then drain off the cooking liquid and reserve. Slice the chicken into 1cm/½in thick strips.

2 Mix together the vegetables, lime leaves and coriander with the peanuts in a bowl and stir in the chicken. Pour over a generous amount of the poaching liquid, so that the salad is quite wet.

3 Using a piece of paper towel dipped in the oil, polish the pieces of banana leaf until shiny.

assembly

Set a piece of banana leaf on each serving plate and heap with the chicken salad. Drizzle over a little extra poaching liquid, and serve.

marinated rump of lamb with sweet potato mash

This delicious combination of sweet mash with pink, tender lamb rump (the cut taken from the top of the leg, also known as boneless chump) makes an excellent alternative to the traditional Sunday lunch. If you can, give the marinade its full 24 hours, to allow the lamb to absorb the flavours; otherwise just rub in the spices extra vigorously. This is a good recipe for the barbecue.

method

1 Score the fat of the lamb in a criss-cross pattern and set aside.

2 Place the chillies, half the coriander leaves, the cinnamon, cardamom, cloves, black peppercorns, turmeric, garlic and salt in a blender or food processor and blend to a paste. Transfer to a shallow bowl and stir in the yoghurt and oil. Spoon the mixture over the lamb, rubbing well to cover all the meat, and set aside for at least 24 hours.

3 Preheat the oven to 180°C/350°F/Gas 4. Bake the sweet potatoes for 40–50 minutes, until soft. Allow to cool slightly, then peel and mash until smooth. Season well and mix in the lemon juice. Keep warm.

4 When ready to cook the lamb, preheat the oven to 200°C/400°F/Gas 6. Brush a heated griddle or heavy-bottomed frying pan with the oil, and sear the lamb, fat-side down, for 5 minutes. Turn and repeat with the underside. Transfer the griddle to the oven and roast the lamb for 15–20 minutes, until just cooked through but still pink inside. Remove from the oven and leave to rest for 5 minutes, then slice each rump into 6 slices.

assembly

Pile a mound of sweet potato mash in the centre of each plate and lay 3 slices of lamb on top. Drizzle a little olive oil around the outside, and serve with wedges of lemon.

ingredients

serves 4

1 *2 rumps of lamb, about 425g/14oz each*

2 marinade
4 red chillies, deseeded
4 tbsp coriander leaves
2 tsp ground cinnamon
1 tsp cardamom pods
1 tsp cloves
2 tsp black peppercorns
1 tsp turmeric
2 garlic cloves
2 tsp sea salt
250ml/8fl oz/1 cup plain yoghurt
1 tbsp vegetable oil

3 *1kg/2lb sweet potatoes*
sea salt
freshly ground black pepper
2 tbsp lemon juice

4 *1 tbsp vegetable oil*

to serve
olive oil to drizzle
1 lemon, quartered

roast saddle of lamb with mushroom tortellini

Although the saddle is the most flavourful, tender cut of lamb, it is not the most economical, as there is a greater proportion of bone to meat. However, if you ask your butcher to bone and roll the cut for you, you'll get quite a good size of joint, and cooked in this simple way, with rosemary and black pepper, it is incomparable.

ingredients

serves 4

1 *2 shallots, finely diced*
1 garlic clove, finely chopped
15g/½oz/1 tbsp unsalted butter
40g/1½oz dried cèpes or porcini
250g/8oz flat mushrooms, diced
2 spring onions, finely chopped
2 tbsp flat-leaf parsley leaves, torn
sea salt
freshly ground black pepper

2 *1 saddle of lamb, boned and rolled*
2 sprigs rosemary
2 tsp vegetable oil
4 tbsp red wine vinegar

3 *4½ tbsp olive oil*
500g/1lb pasta dough (page 213)
semolina flour for dusting
1 egg, beaten

method

1 Sweat the shallots and garlic in the butter over a low heat until soft. Crumble in the dried cèpes, then add the flat mushrooms and simmer for 10 minutes over a medium heat. Remove from the heat, add the spring onions and parsley, and season well with salt and pepper. Drain, reserving the juices, then set aside.

2 Preheat the oven to 220°C/425°F/Gas 7. Season the lamb and rub with the rosemary. Heat a large frying pan with the oil over a high heat, and sear the lamb until golden brown. Transfer to a roasting tin with the rosemary, pour over the vinegar, and roast for about 50–60 minutes, or until cooked through but still pink inside. Leave to rest for 10 minutes.

3 Mix 4 tablespoons of the reserved mushroom juices with 4 tablespoons of the olive oil in a small bowl, and set aside. Roll out the pasta on the finest setting of the pasta machine. Using a cutter or small plate, cut out 4 circles about 15cm/6in in diameter on a surface dusted with semolina flour. Place a mound of the mushroom mixture in the centre of each circle, brush all round with beaten egg, and fold one half of the pasta over the other to create a semi-circle. Wrap this around your forefinger, sealing the corners with a little more beaten egg, and folding over the curved top. Bring a pan of salted water to the boil, add the remaining oil, and cook the tortellini for 3–4 minutes. Remove from the pan and drain.

assembly

Slice the lamb into 4 rounds, and divide between individual plates. Place a tortellini on top of each piece of meat, and drizzle with the combined olive oil and mushroom juices.

leg of rabbit with turnip gratin and mustard

This is a wonderful way to serve up this most maligned of vegetables. Perfectly teamed with the smokiness of roast leg of rabbit, it can also stand its ground alone, with a big green salad on the side.

ingredients

serves 4

1 *500g/1lb turnips, very thinly sliced*

2 *3 tbsp double cream*
  2 tbsp sour cream
  1½ tbsp Dijon mustard
  sea salt
  freshly ground black pepper
  4 spring onions, finely sliced
  60g/2oz/½ cup freshly grated
    Parmesan

3 *4 legs of rabbit, about 250g/8oz*
  each
  2 tsp olive oil

to serve
freshly ground black pepper

method

1 Bring a large pan of water to the boil over a high heat, and blanch the turnips for 30 seconds. Refresh under cold running water, drain and pat dry with paper towels. Set aside.

2 Preheat the oven to 190°C/375°F/Gas 5. Using a whisk, gently combine the double cream, sour cream, mustard, salt and pepper until amalgamated – do not overwhip, as this will cause the cream to separate when cooked. Add the spring onions. Gently fold the turnips into the cream mixture, making sure they are well mixed. Spoon into an ovenproof baking dish, and pack down well. Sprinkle with the Parmesan and bake for 45 minutes. Remove from the oven and keep warm.

3 Increase the oven temperature to 200°C/400°F/Gas 6. Season the rabbit well on both sides and rub with the oil. Heat a griddle or heavy frying pan over a high heat, and cook the rabbit for 4 minutes each side, presentation side first. Remove from the heat, transfer to a baking sheet, and roast in the oven for 8–12 minutes until cooked through. Remove the rabbit from the oven and allow to rest for 5 minutes.

assembly

Serve the rabbit with the gratin in its baking dish. Grind over black pepper to finish.

foie gras and leek terrine

A French speciality from the regions of Alsace Lorraine and Toulouse, foie gras is the rich, velvety-textured liver of a specially fattened goose. Foie gras bought whole are extremely expensive but, as the flavour is so intense, only a small amount is required. You will need to start this recipe two days in advance.

method

1 Devein the foie gras by gently scraping out any surface blood vessels with a sharp knife, and press into a firm, high shape. Lay side by side in a baking tin and season with the mixed spices and salt. Pour over the Armagnac and port, and leave to marinate for 24 hours. The next day, remove the foie gras from the marinade, drain well, and thickly slice into 1cm/½in wedges.

2 Place the leeks in a large cooking pan with the water, oil, thyme, garlic, peppercorns and coriander seeds, and bring to the boil over a medium heat. Simmer for 12–15 minutes until the leeks begin to wilt and soften, then remove from the heat and leave to cool in the pan. When cold, remove the leeks from the liquid with a slotted spoon, and drain on paper towels. Reserve the cooking liquid.

  Preheat the oven to 160°C/325°F/Gas 3. Line the base of a 20cm/8in terrine with a layer of foie gras. Cover with a layer of leeks. Repeat until all the ingredients have been used up, and cover the top with foil. Place the terrine in a roasting tin and pour in enough warm water to come half-way up the sides of the dish. Bake for 35 minutes, then remove from the oven, weigh down with a second terrine dish filled with beans or small weights, and leave in the refrigerator to set for about 12 hours.

3 Whisk together 475ml/16fl oz/2 cups of the leek cooking liquid with the truffle oil. Season with salt and pepper and a squeeze of lemon juice.

assembly

Turn the terrine out on to a large serving plate. Cut into 12 slices, and serve with a drizzle of the truffle oil dressing and toasted brioche.

ingredients

serves 12

1 *3 x 600g/1¼lb lobes of foie gras*
1½ tbsp mixed spices
1 tbsp sea salt
100ml/3½fl oz/scant ½ cup Armagnac
100ml/3½fl oz/scant ½ cup port

2 *6 leeks, dark green leaves removed, scored lengthwise and outer layer removed, roots left on*
475ml/16fl oz/2 cups water
300ml/½ pint/1¼ cups olive oil
5 sprigs thyme
2 garlic cloves
3 peppercorns
6 coriander seeds

3 *2 tbsp truffle oil*
sea salt
freshly ground black pepper
½ lemon

to serve
1 brioche, preferably homemade (page 170) or shop bought, sliced and toasted

peppered sweetbreads on toast

Lamb's sweetbreads are white and tender, with a delicate flavour and texture. As with all sweetbreads, they must be carefully rinsed and refreshed before cooking. Be sure to eat them fresh as they quickly deteriorate.

ingredients

serves 4

1 *500g/1lb lamb's sweetbreads*
¼ celeriac, peeled and cut into
large dice
1 onion, halved
2 sprigs thyme
2 bay leaves
6 peppercorns
pinch of salt

2 *15g/½oz/1 tbsp butter*
30g/1oz celery, finely shredded
40g/1½oz carrots, finely shredded
30g/1oz shallots, finely shredded
30g/1oz cracked black pepper,
sieved several times
2 tbsp redcurrant jelly
2 tbsp malt vinegar
475ml/16fl oz/2 cups beef stock
(page 206)

3 *4 slices brioche, preferably*
homemade (page 170)
60g/2oz/¼ cup butter
2 tbsp olive oil
1 tbsp chopped curly parsley

method

1 Place the sweetbreads in a bowl under cold running water for about 30 minutes to rinse out any blood. Drain, place in a pan with enough water to cover, and bring to the boil. Remove from the heat and refresh under cold running water, then drain again. Return the sweetbreads to the pan, add the vegetables, herbs, peppercorns and salt and enough water to cover, and bring to the boil over a moderate heat. Simmer for 6–8 minutes, then remove from the heat and allow to cool in the liquid. Remove from the pan with a slotted spoon, and set aside. Discard the cooking liquor.

2 Melt the butter in a large pan and sweat the celery, carrots and shallots over a low heat until soft. Add the cracked pepper and cook for 5 minutes. Add the redcurrant jelly and malt vinegar, and reduce until sticky, about 4–5 minutes, then pour in the beef stock and bring to the boil. Simmer for 10 minutes until reduced by half. Remove from the heat and taste for seasoning.

3 Preheat a grill and toast the brioche until golden. Set aside. Heat the butter and olive oil in a large frying pan, and add the sweetbreads. Do not season. Pan-fry until coloured, 4–5 minutes, then remove the sweetbreads and juices from the pan and keep warm. Increase the heat, add the peppered stock and chopped parsley, and bring to the boil. Remove from the heat.

assembly

Place a slice of toasted brioche on each plate and top with the sweetbreads. Drizzle with the peppered sauce.

chargrilled calves' liver with bacon and soft polenta

Whatever your expectations of liver and bacon, prepare to be converted. The secret is in the polenta, which gives a particular sweetness to the dish, and which, ideally, should be timed so that you are cooking the other ingredients while this is still simmering. Otherwise, simply reheat the polenta before serving, adding a little extra cream if it is too dry.

method

1 While the polenta is cooking, heat the vegetable oil in a deep pan and deep-fry the sage leaves for 30 seconds. Remove with a slotted spoon and dry on paper towels. Scatter on a little sea salt.

2 Heat a griddle until just smoking, brush with a little oil, and fry the pancetta until crispy. Remove and keep warm. Add the calves' liver to the griddle and cook for 2–3 minutes on each side, until just cooked through (the inside should still be pink).

assembly

Spoon a mound of polenta into the centre of each plate, lay a slice of liver diagonally across, heap with 3–4 pieces of pancetta, and place a bundle of sage leaves on top.

ingredients

serves 4

1 *750g/1½lb/3 cups polenta (page 213)*
250ml/8fl oz/1 cup vegetable oil
20 sage leaves
sea salt

2 *vegetable oil*
250g/8oz pancetta, thinly sliced,
or smoked streaky bacon
4 slices calves' liver, 150–175g/5–6oz
each, about 5mm/¼in thick

zampone with potatoes and leeks

An Italian speciality from the Modena region, this classic dish must be cooked slowly, and the ingredients allowed to cool in their cooking liquid. Zampone is a pig's trotter, boned and stuffed, available from Italian butchers and delicatessens.

ingredients

serves 4

1 *1 zampone*
1 carrot, sliced lengthwise
1 leek, sliced lengthwise
2 garlic cloves
2 bay leaves
4 sprigs flat-leaf parsley

2 *1 tbsp unsalted butter*
200g/7oz leeks, trimmed and cut
into 10 x 2.5cm/4 x 1in strips
sea salt
freshly ground black pepper
1 litre/1¾ pints/4 cups chicken
stock, preferably homemade
(page 206)
200g/7oz small new potatoes
½ lemon

method

1 Wrap the zampone in foil and place in a large pan. Add the carrot, leek, garlic, bay leaves and parsley, and cover with water. Bring to the boil over a high heat, then reduce the heat and allow to simmer gently for 25–30 minutes. Remove from the heat and leave to cool. With a sharp knife or skewer, puncture the foil around the zampone to allow the cooking liquid to seep inside as it cools.

2 Melt the butter in a small pan over a gentle heat, and sweat the leeks until soft, but not coloured. Season well and remove from the heat. Place the chicken stock and potatoes in a separate pan with seasoning and a squeeze of lemon juice. Bring to the boil, then simmer until the potatoes are almost cooked through. Allow to cool in the stock, then remove the potatoes with a slotted spoon and set aside. Reserve the stock.

assembly

Slice the cooled zampone into 8 pieces, and place in the pan with the chicken stock. Add the potatoes and bring to a simmer over a low heat. Taste for seasoning, and add the leeks. Cook for a further 2 minutes, then remove from the heat and transfer to a large serving bowl.

choucroute garni

Choucroute, the French equivalent of sauerkraut, originated in China during the building of the Great Wall and was introduced to Europe by the invading Tartars, who rather liked this sour dish. Since then it has been dressed up slightly, with sausages and meats added both in the preparation and the serving. This is an ideal recipe for grey winter days, when staying at home and stoking up is the best pastime.

method

1 Heat the goose fat in a large pan. Add the onion, thyme and juniper berries, and sweat over a low heat for 2 minutes. Add the sauerkraut, pork hocks and carrots, and mix well. Cover and simmer for 2 hours, until the pork hocks are cooked through. Remove from the heat and discard the thyme sprigs, juniper berries and carrots. Cut the pork hocks into 4 pieces each and set aside.

2 Return the cooked choucroute to the heat and add the sausages and meats, including the pieces of pork hock. Cover and heat gently for about 20 minutes, until the meats are warmed through.

assembly

Heap the choucroute on to a large serving dish and arrange the sausages, sliced diagonally, and the pieces of pork hock all around.

ingredients

serves 4

1 *60g/2oz goose fat*
1 onion, thinly sliced lengthwise
5 sprigs thyme
1 tbsp juniper berries, tied in a muslin bag
1kg/2lb sauerkraut or pickled cabbage (available from supermarkets and delicatessens)
2 smoked pork hocks
2 carrots, halved lengthwise

2 *4 frankfurters*
4 smoked Toulouse sausages
8 x 2.5cm/1in pieces morteau or Lyonnaise sausage, if available, or chorizo or mortadella

baked mozzarella in prosciutto

Not only does this recipe look fantastic – soft milky cheese wrapped inside salty prosciutto, set in a pool of thick tomato sauce – but it tastes good too. Do not be tempted to stint on either the mozzarella or the ham. Buffalo mozzarella is slightly more expensive than the cow's milk variety, but both taste and texture are noticeably superior. And use only the best quality olive oil.

method

1 Heat 1 tablespoonful of the olive oil in a pan, and sweat the shallot and garlic over a low heat until soft. Add the vinegar and cook for a further 3–4 minutes until reduced, then add the passata and tomatoes, and simmer for 3 minutes. Add the herbs and the remaining olive oil, and cook over a very low heat for 10–15 minutes, stirring occasionally, until thick and a deep red. Season to taste. Remove from the heat, allow to cool, then push through a coarse sieve and set aside.

2 Preheat the oven to 150°C/300°F/Gas 2. Season the mozzarella with black pepper and roll up in the prosciutto, 2 slices per ball of cheese. Heat the oil in a large frying pan over a high heat until just smoking. Place the parcels in the pan and sear, turning constantly, until the outsides are well coloured, about 1 minute. Transfer the parcels to a baking dish and cook in the oven for 5–6 minutes.

assembly

Spoon tomato sauce in the centre of individual plates and sprinkle with the chopped basil and tarragon. Set a mozzarella parcel on top, drizzle with olive oil and serve.

ingredients

serves 4

1 tomato sauce
4 tbsp extra virgin olive oil
1 shallot, finely chopped
1 garlic clove, chopped
1 tbsp Champagne vinegar
125ml/4fl oz/½ cup passata
6 plum tomatoes, peeled and deseeded
5 basil leaves
5 tarragon leaves
sea salt
freshly ground black pepper

2 *4 x 125g/4oz balls buffalo mozzarella*
8 thin slices prosciutto
1½ tbsp vegetable oil

to serve
a little chopped basil and tarragon
olive oil to drizzle

thai pork and pineapple curry with crab

This dish is best prepared over the course of two days for truly sensational results, the anise of the Thai basil providing the perfect foil for the sweetness of the pork and the spice of the curry.

ingredients

serves 4

1 *300g/10oz coconut cream (page 10)*
60g/2oz red curry paste (page 210)
2 tbsp fish sauce
30g/1oz palm sugar
1 tbsp tamarind water (page 217)
600ml/1 pint/2½ cups coconut milk,
  homemade (page 10) or canned
1 pineapple, peeled, cored and cut
  into 2.5cm/1in cubes
5 lime leaves, torn
2 large red chillies, deseeded and
  thinly sliced
2 sticks lemon grass, peeled and cut
  into 2.5cm/1in pieces

2 *1 pork hock*
1 litre/1¾ pints/4 cups water
500g/1lb palm sugar
10 coriander roots, pounded
125ml/4fl oz/½ cup light soy sauce
250ml/8fl oz/1 cup fish sauce

3 *1 red shallot, sliced*
1 tbsp coriander leaves
1 tbsp Thai basil leaves
1 tbsp beansprouts
125g/4oz white crab meat

4 *600ml/1 pint/2½ cups corn oil for*
  deep-frying

method

1 Scrape the fat (the gluey liquid) from the coconut block and place in a large pan over a low heat. Add the curry paste and cook until fragrant, about 30 seconds. Add the coconut block and cook for 2 minutes, breaking it up with the back of a spoon. Add the fish sauce, palm sugar and tamarind water, and simmer until it begins to darken. Add the coconut milk and pineapple, and bring to the boil, stirring constantly. Add the lime leaves, chillies and lemon grass, and cook for a further 3 minutes. Remove from the heat and leave overnight.

2 Preheat the oven to 180°C/350°F/Gas 4. Place the pork hock on a wire rack above a roasting tin and roast for 1½ hours, until the skin is crispy. Remove from the oven and leave to cool. Place the water, palm sugar and coriander roots in a large pan, and bring to the boil, stirring to dissolve the sugar. Boil until reduced by half, about 1 hour. Add the pork hock, the soy sauce and fish sauce, and simmer for a further 2 hours, partially covered, until the liquid forms a syrup. Remove the pork from the pan and drain, reserving the sauce. Allow the pork to cool. Take the meat off the bone, cut into 5cm/2in pieces and set aside. Return the sauce to the boil and simmer until reduced by half.

3 Combine the shallot, coriander, Thai basil and beansprouts in a bowl. Just before serving, mix in the crab meat.

4 Heat the oil in a deep pan until shimmering. Deep-fry the pork until crispy, about 30 seconds. Remove with a slotted spoon and drain on paper towels. Reheat the sauce from the hock pan and pour a little into a shallow bowl. Roll the fried pork pieces in the sauce. Reheat the pineapple curry.

assembly

Heap the crab salad on individual plates and top with 1 or 2 pieces of pork. Drizzle the pork and crab with a little of the warmed sauce, and serve with the warm pineapple curry.

stir-fried pork with chilli paste and snake beans

Snake beans, also called yard-long beans, for obvious reasons, are a thin, peppery type of legume used in Chinese and Thai cooking. Virtually every Asian supermarket sells them but, if they are unavailable, simply substitute green beans and cook for a slightly shorter time. Serve this dish as a starter, perhaps followed by Poached Chicken and Coconut Salad on Banana Leaf (page 116).

method

1 Preheat the oven to 200°C/400°F/Gas 6. Fill a roasting tin with boiling water and balance a wire rack on top. Place the pork on the rack and steam in the oven for 30–40 minutes, until the pork is cooked through and the fat has begun to colour. Remove from the oven and allow to cool, then slice into 4cm/1½in squares.

2 Heat the oil in a wok or frying pan over a high heat. Add the pork and stir well, cooking until it is crisp and brown, about 3–4 minutes. Add the beans, toss well together and cook for 1–2 minutes until hot. Add the chilli paste, stirring well, and cook for a further 1–2 minutes. Remove from the heat and season with fish sauce.

assembly

Tip the pork and beans into a large serving bowl, scatter with the coriander leaves, and serve.

ingredients

serves 4

1 *375g/12oz pork, boned*
   (leg or shoulder)

2 *1 tsp vegetable oil*
   4 snake/yard-long beans, cut into
      7cm/3in lengths, or 125g/4oz
      green beans
   1 tbsp chilli paste (page 209)
   1 tsp fish sauce, or to taste

to serve
2 tbsp coriander leaves

escalope of veal with egg and parmesan

Dipped in a light batter before frying, the veal in this recipe is substantial enough to be served alone, with just a little rocket salad for accompaniment. Serve it as a winter lunch, or a main course at supper. Pork fillets can be used in place of the veal.

ingredients

serves 4

1 *2 medium eggs*
4 canned anchovies, finely chopped
175g/6oz/1 cup freshly grated
*   Parmesan*
2 tbsp chopped flat-leaf parsley
½ tsp freshly ground black pepper

2 *60g/2oz rocket*
4 tbsp olive oil
freshly ground black pepper

3 *4 tbsp vegetable oil*
4 escalopes of veal, 125g/4oz each
60g/2oz/½ cup plain flour
60g/2oz/¼ cup butter
2 tsp white wine vinegar

to serve
rocket salad (optional)
1 lemon, quartered

method

1 Whisk the eggs for 1 minute until light. Stir in the anchovies, Parmesan, parsley and black pepper.

2 Place the rocket in the bottom of a shallow serving dish and dress with the olive oil and black pepper.

3 Heat a large frying pan over a high heat and add the vegetable oil. Turn the veal in the flour until evenly coated, then dip in the egg mixture. Place the escalopes in the pan over a high heat and cook for 1 minute. Reduce the heat to medium and cook for a further 2 minutes until golden on the underside. Turn and cook the other side for 2–3 minutes. Add the butter. When it has melted, pour in the vinegar, tilting the pan to ensure the juices combine, and remove the escalopes.

assembly

Lay the escalopes on the dressed rocket and drizzle with the melted butter from the pan. Serve with extra rocket salad if liked, and lemon wedges.

fillet of beef with bone marrow and parmesan

There is nothing quite like the mellow sweetness of bone marrow, but it can be quite difficult to get hold of, so it is advisable to order the bones in advance from a reputable organic butcher.

method

1 Place the marrow bones in a shallow bowl and cover with the iced water. Leave to steep, preferably overnight, to allow the blood to seep out. Alternatively, scrub the bones with a small brush, and run under cold water until clean.

2 Using your forefinger – taking care to avoid the sharp inside edges – or the handle of a wooden spoon, push out the marrow from 4 of the bones and chop roughly. Place in a small bowl or mortar with the Parmesan, and pound to a smooth paste. Stir in the butter and mix well.

3 Preheat the oven to 200°C/400°F/Gas 6. Scrape clean the remaining pieces of marrow bone with a sharp knife while still wet, and set aside. Place a frying pan or griddle over a medium heat until smoking. Season the beef fillets and rub with a little olive oil. Place the fillets in the pan and sear for 3–4 minutes on each side until browned, adding the marrow bones for the last 2 minutes to colour the bones. Transfer the fillets and bones to a roasting tin, and place in the oven for 6–8 minutes. Remove and allow to rest for at least 5 minutes.

4 Bring the chicken stock to the boil and simmer until reduced by half. Lower the heat and whisk in a small amount of the marrow and Parmesan paste. Repeat, a little at a time, until all the paste has been incorporated, then remove from the heat. Add the rocket and allow it to wilt slightly, about 30 seconds, then remove with a slotted spoon.

assembly

Place the beef fillets on top of the toasted croûtons, if using, and heap with the wilted rocket. Dip the roasted marrow bones in the sauce to glaze, and set one on top of each fillet. Circle with the sauce and serve.

ingredients

serves 4

1 *8 marrow bones, 5cm/2in long*
1.25 litres/2 pints/5 cups iced water

2 *60g/2oz/½ cup freshly grated*
   Parmesan
60g/2oz/¼ cup butter

3 *4 fillets of beef, 175g/6oz each*
sea salt
freshly ground black pepper
1 tbsp olive oil

4 *175ml/6fl oz/scant ¾ cup chicken*
   stock, preferably homemade
   (page 206)
90g/3oz rocket

to serve
4 small rounds of toasted white
   bread (optional)

leaves and herbs

With the improved range and quality of imported foods, and a growing interest in far-flung cuisines, the market for salad leaves and fresh herbs has changed almost beyond recognition in recent years. Not so long ago, the only leaf a supermarket shelf had to offer would be a tired old iceberg lettuce, or perhaps a bunch of curly parsley or two, but these days even reaching for the most straightforward pot of basil sends you rooting through its more exotic neighbours, such as lemon grass, fenugreek or mustard leaf. Similarly, the once-familiar old leathery spinach has been replaced with younger, smaller-leaf versions, and alternatives such as rocket, endive, Chinese cabbage and radicchio do battle with the iceberg at every turn. Even spring greens, the vitamin-packed leaves of the early crops once dismissed as pig fodder, have found their way to the forefront, their bitter flavours and crunchy texture a perfect accompaniment to garlicky spaghetti or wok-fried salad leaves.

With such widespread innovation on the part of supermarket buyers, it is only appropriate that new recipes should reflect this: why not test the waters with Grilled Radicchio with Tomato Vinaigrette and Goat's Cheese, or perhaps an Endive Salad with Smoked Bacon and Mustard Dressing, or maybe even the spicy Wok-fried Spinach with Sweet Potatoes and Chilli Jam? You won't look back.

mibuna leaves

grilled radicchio with tomato vinaigrette and goat's cheese

The bitterness of the radicchio combined with the sweetness of the goat's cheese makes this a great dish for revitalizing jaded tastebuds. If possible, buy radicchio treviso, the longer, leafier kind, as it is much less dense than the usual round type. But if you cannot find this, don't worry: simply cut the radicchio into quarters and grill for a little longer.

ingredients

serves 6

1 *125ml/4fl oz/½ cup olive oil*
625g/1¼ lb very ripe tomatoes,
roughly chopped
1 tbsp passata or puréed tomatoes
12 tarragon leaves, torn
1 sprig flat-leaf parsley, chopped
½ lemon
½ tbsp sea salt
freshly ground black pepper
1 tbsp white wine vinegar
caster sugar to taste (optional)

2 *3 heads radicchio treviso*
juice of 1 lemon
4 tbsp olive oil

3 *90g/3oz marjoram*
300g/10oz goat's cheese, crumbled

to serve
olive oil to drizzle (optional)
pain de campagne (page 163)

method

1 Heat 3 tablespoonfuls of the olive oil in a pan. Add the tomatoes and passata, and cook over a high heat for 3–4 minutes. Add the herbs and the lemon half (in one piece) and season well with the sea salt and black pepper. Bring to a rolling boil, then reduce the heat and simmer for 1–2 minutes. Reduce the heat further and add the remaining oil and the vinegar. Simmer for 25–30 minutes and season to taste, adding a little sugar if the tomatoes are too sharp.

2 Meanwhile, remove the outer leaves of the radicchio and slice in half lengthwise. Lay core up in a baking dish, drizzle with the lemon juice and sprinkle with salt and pepper. Pour over the olive oil and leave for 10 minutes to marinate.

3 Heat a griddle or frying pan over a high heat until smoking. Lay the radicchio halves core down and cook for 3–4 minutes, until the leaves are blackened and wilted. Turn and cook for a further 3–4 minutes. Remove from the heat and arrange in an ovenproof serving dish with the marjoram and the goat's cheese. Preheat the grill and place the dish under it for 2–3 minutes until the cheese is just browned.

assembly

Spoon the tomato vinaigrette over the radicchio, drizzle with a little extra olive oil if liked, and serve at room temperature with plenty of pain de campagne to mop up the dressing.

stir-fried asian greens with ginger and oyster sauce

Three different types of cabbage, bok choi, choi sum and Chinese cabbage (also known as sui choi) form the basis of an infinite number of soup, chow mein and noodle dishes. Bok choi, one of the oldest Chinese leaves, has been cultivated in the East since the fifth century and, along with many other Asian greens, is increasingly popular in Europe and North America for its sweet, sharp flavour and tender stems. Simply prepared using ginger and oyster sauce, this recipe is the perfect way to enjoy Asian greens. It is swiftly cooked so as not to lose any flavour, and eaten either as a side dish, or as a course in its own right.

ingredients

**serves 4 as a starter
or 8 as an accompaniment**
1 500g/1lb bok choi, stems and
   leaves cut in half lengthwise
   500g/1lb choi sum, stems and leaves
   cut in half lengthwise
   250g/8oz Chinese cabbage, cut into
   10cm/4in shreds
   1 tbsp sesame oil
   60g/2oz root ginger, peeled and cut
   into julienne strips
   3 garlic cloves, chopped
   125ml/4fl oz/½ cup oyster sauce
   1 long red chilli, deseeded and cut
   into julienne strips

method

1 Toss the bok choi, choi sum and Chinese cabbage together. Heat a wok or frying pan over a high heat and add the sesame oil, ginger and garlic. Stir and immediately throw in the greens. Cook over a high heat, moving the wok constantly, for 2–3 minutes. Add the oyster sauce and chilli, toss for 1–2 minutes until the oyster sauce is warmed through, then remove from the heat and cover the wok with a lid or piece of foil for 2 minutes, to allow the greens to rest.

assembly

Transfer to a large bowl and serve immediately, while hot.

thai cabbage salad with soy

Reading the list of ingredients for this salad, you might easily wonder where exactly the Thai part originated: Chinese leaves, Chinese soy sauce, Chinese rice vinegar, coriander (first used in China), peanuts (native to Brazil), chillies (Latin American) and cucumbers (everywhere). But frankly, once you've tasted it you'll be so impressed you won't care about such pedantry.

ingredients

serves 4

1 *½ head Chinese leaves, thinly shredded*
¼ cucumber, deseeded and sliced
2 spring onions, thinly sliced diagonally
125g/4oz beansprouts

2 *4 tbsp peanut oil*
2 tbsp Chinese rice vinegar
½ tsp caster sugar
1 tsp light soy sauce
½ garlic clove, finely chopped
½ red chilli, deseeded and finely diced

3 *1 tbsp coriander leaves*

to serve
60g/2oz/⅓ cup skinned, unsalted roasted peanuts, crushed

method

1 Place the shredded Chinese leaves in a large bowl with the cucumber, spring onions and beansprouts.

2 Combine the oil, vinegar, sugar, soy sauce, garlic and red chilli, and pour over the raw vegetables. Mix well, then leave for 15 minutes to marinate.

3 Just before serving, toss in the coriander leaves.

assembly

Transfer the salad to a large serving bowl, sprinkle with the crushed roasted peanuts and serve immediately.

wok-fried spinach with sweet potatoes and chilli jam

Spicy and mellow at the same time, this is a perfect accompaniment for noodles or roast meat. Any leftovers can be eaten cold, straight from the fridge.

method

1 Preheat the oven to 180°C/350°F/Gas 4. Bake the sweet potatoes for 40–50 minutes, or until cooked through. Set aside until cool enough to handle, then peel and cut into large chunks, about 2.5cm/1in thick.

2 Heat a wok with the oil until just sizzling, then stir in the chilli jam, standing back as it will spit, and cook for 30 seconds. Add the sweet potato chunks and the spring onions, and toss well for 1–2 minutes. Add the spinach, pressing down well and stirring to ensure that the chilli jam is thoroughly dispersed. Cook for 2–3 minutes until the spinach begins to wilt, then remove from the heat and check for seasoning.

assembly

Spoon into a large bowl and serve.

ingredients

serves 4

1 *4 medium sweet potatoes*

2 *1 tsp vegetable oil*
1 tbsp chilli jam (page 209)
2 spring onions, finely sliced
    diagonally
300g/10oz spinach, rinsed
sea salt
freshly ground black pepper

spinach salad with soft-boiled eggs and anchovies

A variation on the classic Caesar salad, this version has all the qualities to succeed: snappy dressing, plenty of bite, and charm oozing thick from the soft-boiled eggs. The dressing can be stored in the refrigerator for up to a week.

method

1 Bring a large pan of water to the boil and add the salt. Allow to dissolve, then gently lower in the eggs, adding half a cup of cold water at the same time, to help prevent the eggs cracking. Cook for 5 minutes, then cool under cold running water, and shell.

2 Wash the spinach very gently so as not to bruise the leaves. Allow to drain.

3 Place the raw eggs, mustard, vinegar and half the anchovies in a food processor or blender and process for 2–3 minutes until white. Slowly add the olive oil in a thin stream until it is amalgamated. Season with salt and pepper to taste, adding a little warm water if the dressing is too thick. Don't worry if it tastes very salty at this stage, for the spinach will absorb this.

assembly

Place the spinach in a large bowl and toss with the dressing. Arrange the soft-boiled eggs and remaining anchovies on top, and finish with a grinding of black pepper.

ingredients

serves 4

1 *½ tsp salt*
8 medium eggs

2 *375g/12oz young leaf spinach*

3 *2 medium eggs*
4 tsp Dijon mustard
125ml/4fl oz/½ cup wine vinegar
125g/4oz canned anchovies
600ml/1 pint/2½ cups olive oil
sea salt
freshly ground black pepper

to serve
freshly ground black pepper

jt's caesar salad

A classic salad given a new identity with JT's own dressing, this is quick to prepare and perfect for light lunches, or as an accompaniment to grilled chicken or salmon. It is even speedier to make if you keep a bottle of the dressing in the refrigerator, and a jar of homemade croûtons in your store cupboard.

ingredients

serves 4

1 1 medium egg
1 egg yolk
1 tbsp Dijon mustard
1 tbsp shallot vinegar
1 garlic clove, crushed
200ml/7fl oz/scant 1 cup
   vegetable oil
200ml/7fl oz/scant 1 cup olive oil
175g/6oz/1½ cups cups freshly
   grated Parmesan
2 anchovy fillets, finely chopped

2 100g/3½oz pancetta, cut into lardons
2 thick slices white bread
2 tbsp olive oil

3 4 Little Gem lettuces, leaves
   separated, or 1 large cos or
   romaine lettuce, leaves torn into
   large pieces

to serve

60g/2oz anchovy fillets, cut in half
   lengthwise
60g/2oz/½ cup shaved Parmesan
freshly ground black pepper

method

1 Whisk the egg, egg yolk, mustard, vinegar and garlic in a large bowl until the mixture begins to thicken and turn pale. Slowly add the oils, whisking constantly, until well amalgamated. Add a little hot water if the mixture seems too thick. Stir in 150g/5oz/1¼ cups of the grated Parmesan and the chopped anchovies, and set aside.

2 Heat a frying pan over a moderate heat and fry the pancetta until crisp. Drain on paper towels. Cut the bread into chunks and fry in the bacon fat in the pan, adding a little olive oil if necessary, until golden brown. Remove from the heat and add the remaining 25g/1oz/¼ cup grated Parmesan. Toss well, then set aside.

3 Place the lettuce leaves in a bowl and toss with the dressing to coat thoroughly.

assembly

Divide the dressed lettuce between 4 plates and scatter with the croûtons and pancetta. Arrange the anchovy fillets on top, and finish with the shaved Parmesan and a grinding of black pepper.

sweet basil salad with fennel, coriander and chilli

Fennel, with its aromatic anise flavour, is a strong influence in this Thai-inspired recipe, combining well with both the hot chillies and cool herbs. A wonderful accompaniment to grilled fish.

method

1 Mix the fennel with 1 tablespoon of the lime juice and the salt, and set aside for 30 minutes.

2 Warm the olive oil in a small frying pan, then add the chillies and the spring onions. Toss for 30 seconds, then remove from the heat and add the remaining lime juice. Set aside for 30 minutes. Combine the marinated fennel with the chillies and spring onions, and stir well. Season with salt and pepper, and the extra lime juice to taste.

3 Place the coriander, basil and mint leaves in a large bowl and toss together.

assembly

Fold the coriander, basil and mint into the fennel and chillies, and transfer to a large serving dish.

ingredients

serves 4

1 *1 fennel bulb, finely shaved, ideally on a mandolin*
2 tbsp freshly squeezed lime juice
½ tsp sea salt

2 *4 tbsp olive oil*
2 red chillies, deseeded and cut into julienne strips
4 spring onions, finely sliced diagonally
sea salt
freshly ground black pepper

3 *2 tbsp coriander leaves*
2 tbsp basil leaves
1 tbsp mint leaves

thai herb salad with chilli and lime dressing

A distinctive and aromatic salad, this combines the anise flavour of Thai basil with the grassiness of coriander and the coolness of fresh mint in a sharp and tangy dressing. Don't worry if you can't find pak chee laos. This is simply a variety of coriander grown north-east of Thailand and can be left out without the salad suffering a great deal. If you are lucky enough to find it, however, it will be worth the hunt, for its flavour is quite unique and gives just that extra kick to the dish.

ingredients

serves 4

1 ½ red chilli, deseeded and roughly
chopped
2 small green chillies, roughly
chopped
1 garlic clove
¼ tsp sea salt
40g/1½oz palm sugar
1 tbsp freshly squeezed lime juice
2 tbsp fish sauce
2 tbsp sake

2 30g/1oz cucumber, deseeded and
cut into julienne strips
60g/2oz pak chee laos (optional)
60g/2oz coriander
60g/2oz Thai basil
60g/2oz mint
30g/1oz spring onions, finely
sliced diagonally
15g/½oz lemon grass, peeled and
thinly sliced
15g/½oz Thai shallots, thinly sliced

method

1 Using a mortar and pestle, crush the chillies and garlic in the salt. Add the sugar and pound to a paste. Add the lime juice, fish sauce and sake, and set aside.

2 Combine the cucumber with the herbs. Mix the spring onions, lemon grass and shallots with a little of the dressing. Toss the cucumber and spring onion mixtures together, and fold in a little more of the dressing.

assembly

Transfer to a serving bowl and drizzle with extra dressing.

endive salad with smoked bacon and mustard dressing

Although endive, or chicory, is an extremely common salad ingredient in France, it has yet to really catch on elsewhere, despite the fact that it is available all year round, holds its shape better than ordinary lettuces, and has a bitter taste that makes it the perfect companion for similarly strong flavours such as bacon or mustard. Do not confuse it with the curly endive lettuce, which is quite different.

method

1 Whisk together the mustard and vinegar, and slowly add the oils, blending well. Fold in the single cream and set aside.

2 Preheat the grill and cook the bacon until crispy. Toss the endive leaves in a bowl with the mustard dressing.

assembly

Place the dressed endive on individual plates and lay 2 rashers of bacon over the top of each one. Sprinkle with chopped chives and serve with a grinding of black pepper.

ingredients

serves 4

1 *6 tbsp Dijon mustard*
4 tbsp white wine vinegar
90ml/3fl oz/⅓ cup hazelnut oil
90ml/3fl oz/⅓ cup peanut oil
150ml/¼ pint/⅔ cup single cream

2 *175g/6oz smoked streaky bacon*
3 endives, leaves separated

to serve
2 tbsp chopped chives
freshly ground black pepper

mezzo herb salad with octopus

With its faintly lobster-like flavour, octopus is a perfect companion for the aromatic combination of herb and lemon dressing. Allow 24 hours for the octopus to marinate, to ensure the flesh is tender, and never prepare the dressing more than 2 hours in advance or it will lose its flavour.

method

1 Bring a pan of salted water to the boil and blanch the octopus for 30 seconds. Remove and drain well. Split the heads but leave the bodies intact. Place in a bowl and leave to cool.

2 Place the lemon juice, lemon, water, oil, garlic, thyme and coriander seeds in a pan, and bring to the boil. Remove from the heat and pour the marinade over the octopus. Leave to marinate for 24 hours.

3 Place the salad herbs, chilli and spring onions in a large bowl and toss well. Drain the octopus and cut into 5cm/2in strips. Add to the herb mixture and combine thoroughly.

4 Whisk together the olive oil, lemon juice and black pepper to taste, and pour over the herbs and octopus.

assembly

Toss the salad well and divide between 4 shallow bowls. Serve immediately.

ingredients

serves 4

1 *sea salt*
500g/1lb baby octopus (polpito),
   about 30g/1oz each

2 marinade
60ml/2fl oz/¼ cup lemon juice
½ lemon, diced
125ml/4fl oz/½ cup water
125ml/4fl oz/½ cup olive oil
1 garlic clove
2 sprigs thyme
10 coriander seeds, crushed

3 salad
20g/¾oz sage
30g/1oz coriander
10g/⅓oz tarragon
30g/1oz basil
20g/¾oz red mustard
20g/¾oz chilli, diced
20g/¾oz spring onions, finely
   sliced diagonally

4 dressing
300ml/½ pint/1¼ cups olive oil
4 tbsp lemon juice
freshly ground black pepper

flour and yeast

Staple ingredients in virtually every carbohydrate-based diet, flour and yeast are the stock in trade of bakers and breadmakers the world over. Dough for breads and pizzas, pastries for pies, and sponges for cakes: all centre upon these two ingredients, and hence form an important part of every international cuisine. Sadly, however, in domestic kitchens, freshly made breads, cakes and pastries have become less common. With the rise of good delicatessens and supermarkets, it is significantly easier to buy a loaf of bread, or tart case, than to make one, and many home cooks are forgetting the inherent satisfaction in doing this for themselves.

And with that loss of tradition comes loss of confidence; how many accomplished cooks claim they simply don't dare to make bread, for it never works, is too time-consuming and tastes better bought from the shop on the corner? All are good excuses, but none of them is a worthy reason. For whatever the physical perfection of a store-bought item, with its straight edges and even rise, the texture and flavour of home baking simply cannot be improved upon. Of course, few people have the time to bake every day, but once in a while, treat yourself: allow an extra half hour to make your own pastry, or an extra hour to knock up a loaf of bread — you'd spend that time queuing at the supermarket, anyway.

pissaladière with rocket

Pissaladière, a Provençal-style pizza made with bread dough, onions and anchovies, is believed to have been introduced into French cuisine by the Romans. There are many versions, some using a thick tomato and garlic sauce, others using puff pastry instead of dough. In this recipe, the emphasis is on the sweetness of the caramelized onions, balancing the sharper tang of anchovy and black olive. Pizza has never tasted so good.

ingredients

serves 4–6

1 *60g/2oz/¼ cup unsalted butter*
1kg/2lb onions, sliced top to bottom
30g/1oz thyme leaves
2 tbsp red wine vinegar

2 *pizza dough (page 214)*
flour for dusting

3 *60g/2oz canned anchovies,*
  halved lengthwise
90g/3oz/1⅔ cups pitted black olives
30g/1oz thyme sprigs, leaves picked
freshly ground black pepper
olive oil for brushing

4 *2 tbsp red wine vinegar*
1 tbsp Dijon mustard
sea salt
freshly ground black pepper
125ml/4fl oz/½ cup extra virgin
  olive oil
1 tsp walnut oil
175g/6oz rocket

method

1 Melt the butter in a large pan over a medium heat until lightly browned. Add the onions and thyme, and stir to coat with the butter. Add the red wine vinegar and continue stirring, scraping the sides and bottom of the pan with a wooden spoon to keep all the flavours, until the onions are caramelized and dry, about 35–40 minutes. Remove from the heat and leave to cool.

2 Preheat the oven to 200°C/400°F/Gas 6. Roll out the pizza dough on a lightly floured surface into a large circle about 5mm/¼in thick. Drape over the rolling pin and place on a baking sheet dusted with flour. Spread the caramelized onions over the dough, leaving an outside margin of about 2.5cm/1in.

3 Lay the anchovies across the onions in a criss-cross pattern. Place 2 black olives in the centre of each diamond, sprinkle with thyme leaves and grind with black pepper. Bake in the oven for 20–25 minutes, until the crust is golden brown and risen. Brush with olive oil to finish.

4 Whisk the vinegar, mustard, salt and pepper in a bowl and slowly pour in the oils. Pour over the rocket and toss well.

assembly

Pile the pissaladière with the dressed rocket and serve.

fougasses

A Provençal flat bread, fougasse is traditionally served on Christmas Eve, and forms the core of thirteen different desserts, said to symbolize Christ and the twelve disciples. Best eaten straight from the oven, warm and scented, it is delicious served with fresh and dried fruits and cheese, and makes an excellent breakfast bread at any time of year.

ingredients

serves 6

1 15g/½oz fresh yeast, or 7g/¼oz dried yeast
90ml/3fl oz/⅓ cup lukewarm water
750g/1½lb/6 cups unbleached white bread flour, plus extra for dusting
175g/6oz/¾ cup caster sugar
1½ tsp salt

2 shredded rind and juice of 1 large orange
90ml/3fl oz/⅓ cup olive oil, plus extra for greasing and brushing
2 medium eggs, lightly beaten

3 90g/3oz/⅓ cup candied orange and lemon peel

method

1 Blend the fresh yeast with the water, or the dried yeast, if using, with the water and 1 teaspoonful of the sugar, and set aside. Place the flour, sugar and salt in a large bowl, mix thoroughly, and make a well in the centre. Pour in the yeast liquid, stirring in enough of the flour from the sides to form a batter, and leave to stand in a warm place for 10 minutes.

2 In a separate bowl, combine the orange rind and juice with the oil and beaten eggs, then gently stir into the yeast batter. Work in the flour using your fingertips, adding a little extra water if the dough is too dry, or extra flour if it is too wet. Turn out the dough on to a floured board and knead until smooth, about 8–10 minutes. Place in a greased bowl, cover with a damp cloth, and leave in a warm place to prove until doubled in size, about 1 hour.

3 Gently knock back the risen dough using your fist, and turn out again on to a floured board. Knead in the candied peel until evenly mixed, 3–4 minutes, then divide the dough into 6 equal-sized pieces. Roll out each piece into an oval about 30 x 20cm/12 x 8in and 1cm/½in thick. Using the point of a sharp knife, cut 9–10 diagonal short slits on either side of the dough, forming a herringbone design, and place, well spaced, on floured baking sheets. Leave to rise again in a warm place, covered with damp cloths, until almost doubled in size, about 1 hour.

   Preheat the oven to 200°C/400°F/Gas 6. Brush the fougasses with a little olive oil, and bake for 18–20 minutes until lightly golden. Transfer to a wire rack to cool, and eat the same day.

potato pancakes with crème fraîche and caviar

Caviar, the salted roe of sturgeon, has long been considered the height of indulgence but, in this recipe, it need not break the bank. There are three types of black caviar, Beluga, Osietr and Sevruga, considered by connoisseurs to be infinitely superior to the cheaper versions made from the eggs of the cod, catfish, mullet, shad or whiting. Unless you're an expert on caviar, however, these will work just as well.

method

1 Bring a pan of salted water to the boil and cook the potatoes until tender. Drain well and put through a fine mouli or food processor until smooth. Bring the milk to the boil in a large pan, add the potato and mix well. Lower the heat, stir in the potato flour, and slowly incorporate the whole eggs, beating constantly, then the egg white. Still beating, add the cream and season well. Remove from the heat.

2 In a small frying pan, about 15cm/6in in diameter, melt a little of the butter over a low heat. Add 1 large tablespoonful of the potato and cream mixture, enough to fill half the pan, and flatten out into a round. Increase the heat to medium and cook for about 4 minutes. Turn over, and cook for another 4 minutes until the pancake is golden brown, and the inside is cooked through when tested with the point of a knife. Repeat until you have used all the mixture, adding more butter as necessary. The pancakes may be reheated, but should not be refrigerated.

assembly

Place the warm pancakes on serving plates and top each one with a good dessertspoonful of crème fraîche and a sprinkling of chives and caviar.

ingredients

serves 4

1 *sea salt*
   300g/10oz potatoes, peeled and cut into chunks
   100ml/3½fl oz/generous ⅓ cup milk
   20g/¾oz/2½ tbsp potato flour
   2 medium eggs
   1 egg white
   2 tsp single cream
   freshly ground black pepper

2 *125g/4oz/½ cup unsalted butter*

to serve

200ml/7fl oz/scant 1 cup crème fraîche
30g/1oz chives, chopped
100g/3½oz caviar

161

pain de campagne

Making bread using a starter results in a slightly acidic, yeasty loaf that tastes better than more speedily produced breads and is more easily digested. Because the dough goes through three stages rather than two, it has a much stronger flavour, with a finer crust and texture. If you are a regular bread-maker, you can cut out the starter stage by always keeping back 60g/2oz of the prepared dough, and adding this to your next batch of dough.

method

1 Sift the flour into a bowl, add the water and yeast, and whisk until a smooth batter forms. Cover with a tea towel and leave to rise in a warm place for at least 2 hours, preferably overnight.

2 Whisk together the water and yeast in a small bowl, and leave to stand for 5 minutes until frothy. Sift the flours into a mixing bowl with the salt, and add the yeast mixture. Stir in the starter and blend well. Shape into a ball, turn out on to a floured board, and knead for 12–15 minutes until the dough is smooth and elastic. Add a little extra flour if the dough becomes sticky, and a few drops of water if it is too dry. Shape into a ball and place in a lightly greased bowl. Cover and leave in a warm place for about 2 hours, or until doubled in size.

3 Knock back the dough with your fist, then turn out on to a floured board and knead for 3–4 minutes. Shape the dough into a ball and place on a floured baking sheet. Cover with a tea towel and leave to rise in a warm place for another 1–1½ hours, or until the dough doubles in size.

  Preheat the oven to 220°C/425°F/Gas 7. Sprinkle the top of the dough with a little flour, and, using a sharp knife, make 6 shallow slits on the top, 3 in each direction. Fill a roasting tin with hot water and place on the floor of the oven: this creates a damp atmosphere which results in a better crust. Bake the bread in the oven for 30 minutes. Remove the tin of water and reduce the heat to 200°C/400°F/Gas 6. Bake for another 15 minutes, until the crust is golden brown and well risen, and the bread sounds hollow when tapped on the base. Transfer to a wire rack to cool.

ingredients

makes 1 loaf

1 starter
200g/7oz/1¾ cups unbleached strong white bread flour
175ml/6fl oz/scant ¾ cup lukewarm water
5g/¼oz fresh yeast, or ½ tsp dried yeast

2 *90ml/3fl oz/⅓ cup lukewarm water*
5g/¼oz fresh yeast, or ½ tsp dried yeast
200g/7oz/1¾ cups unbleached strong white bread flour, plus extra for dusting
45g/1½ oz/6 tbsp rye flour
1 tsp salt
butter for greasing

3 *2–3 tbsp unbleached strong white bread flour*

olive and semolina bread

Fruity and rich, this is the perfect bread for summer picnics, eaten with Greek Salad (page 75) or Tomato Tart (page 71). It also tastes delicious toasted next day with a little olive oil for dipping. Allow time to make the fermented dough starter, as this is what gives the bread its depth of flavour.

ingredients

makes 1 loaf

1 starter
200g/7oz/1¾ cups unbleached
   strong white flour
5g/¼oz fresh yeast, or ½ tsp
   dried yeast
125ml/4fl oz/½ cup lukewarm
   water

2 200g/7oz/1¾ cups unbleached
   strong white flour, plus extra
   for dusting
5g/¼oz fresh yeast, or ½ tsp dried
   yeast
1 tsp salt
575ml/18fl oz/2¼ cups cold water
2 tbsp olive oil
150g/5oz/1 cup pitted black olives
1 tbsp chopped fresh rosemary
   leaves
butter for greasing

3 60g/2oz/⅓ cup semolina flour

method

1 Sift the flour into a large bowl and make a well in the centre. Whisk the yeast into the water and leave until frothy, 4–5 minutes. Pour the yeast into the well and mix in a food processor, using a dough hook on slow speed, for 5 minutes. Alternatively, mix by hand, drawing the flour into the liquid little by little, until a smooth dough is formed. Cover with a clean cloth and leave in a warm place to prove for 8–12 hours, or overnight.

2 Sift the flour into a mixing bowl and add the yeast, salt, cold water and olive oil. Mix in a food processor, using a dough hook on medium speed, for 4 minutes, or by hand, until the dough is smooth. Transfer to a floured board and knead for 8–10 minutes until the dough is smooth and elastic. Add the starter and continue kneading for a further 3–4 minutes until well combined. Add the olives and rosemary, and knead to combine. Place the dough in a greased bowl, cover with a clean cloth, and leave in a warm place for 1–1½ hours, until doubled in size.

3 Preheat the oven to 230°/450°F/Gas 8. Shape the dough into a rectangular loaf and score the corners to add decoration. Dust with half the semolina flour. Scatter the remaining semolina flour on a baking sheet and place the dough on top. Bake for 15 minutes, then reduce the temperature to 200°C/400°F/Gas 6 and bake for another 35–40 minutes, or until the bread is brown and well risen, and sounds hollow when tapped on the base. Transfer to a wire rack to cool.

ficelle

A classic French bread, the ficelle is a variation on the baguette, using exactly the same dough and shaping methods, but in smaller quantities, so as to create a much thinner, crustier loaf.

method

1 Whisk the yeast with 125ml/4fl oz/½ cup of the water and leave until frothy, 4–5 minutes. Add the salt to the flour and sift into a large mixing bowl. Make a well in the centre and pour in the yeast mixture and the remaining water. Gently mix the flour into the liquid until a dough begins to form, then turn out on to a floured board or surface and knead for 10–15 minutes until smooth and elastic. Shape the dough into a ball, return to the bowl, and leave to rise in a warm place, covered with a damp cloth, for 1 hour.

Remove the dough from the bowl and knead on a floured board for 2 minutes. Divide the dough in half and form each half into a sausage about 12cm/5in long. Roll out one sausage, working back and forth to elongate the dough, until it forms a long, thin baguette shape, 35cm/14in long. Transfer to a floured baking sheet and repeat with the other sausage. Leave for another 30 minutes to prove, or until doubled in size.

Preheat the oven to 230°C/450°F/Gas 8. Fill a small tin with water and place in the bottom of the oven to create the damp heat best suited to French bread. Make shallow, diagonal cuts on the tops of the loaves and bake for 15 minutes. Remove the tin of water, reduce the temperature to 200°C/400°F/Gas 6, and bake for another 10–12 minutes, or until the bread is golden brown and a good crust has formed. Serve immediately.

ingredients

makes 2 loaves

1 *20g/¾ oz fresh yeast, or 1 tbsp dried yeast*
250ml/8fl oz/1 cup lukewarm water
1½ tsp sea salt
375g/12oz/3 cups unbleached plain white flour, plus extra for dusting

crostini

Crostini make wonderful store-cupboard staples for serving with soup, or topping with tapenade or fresh tomatoes.

method

1 Mix the garlic and salt with the olive oil until they form a paste. Rub the mixture over the crust of the baguette until well absorbed. Cover and set aside for 24 hours.

   Preheat the oven to 220°C/425°F/Gas 7. Thinly slice the baguette on the bias about 1cm/½in thick, and place on a baking sheet. Bake in the oven for 5–6 minutes until lightly coloured and crisp. Allow to cool, then store in large air-tight jars until ready to use.

ingredients

makes 10–12 crostini

1 1 garlic clove, crushed
   ½ tsp salt
   2 tsp olive oil
   ½ stale baguette or ficelle (page 165)

grissini

These long thin dough sticks are perfect for dipping in sauces.

method

1 Sift the flours into a mixing bowl and make a hole in the centre. Mix the yeast with the water and pour into the flour with the olive oil and salt. Using a dough hook, mix in a food processor on medium speed for about 10 minutes, then transfer to a floured board and knead for 5 minutes. Alternatively, draw the flour into the liquid and mix by hand for 12–15 minutes until the dough is elastic and smooth, then transfer to a board and knead as above. Cover and leave to rest in a warm place for 45 minutes.

   Preheat the oven to 230°C/450°F/Gas 8. Divide the dough into 8 pieces and roll out into long sticks on a floured board. Place on a baking sheet and press the ends down to prevent them shrinking during cooking. Bake in the oven for about 12 minutes, until golden brown.

Ingredients

makes 8 grissini

1 200g/7oz/1¾ cups unbleached strong white flour, plus extra for dusting
   200g/7oz/1¾ cups '00' flour (baker's flour)
   10g/⅓oz/2 tsp fresh yeast, or 1 tsp dried yeast
   200ml/7fl oz/scant 1 cup water
   2 tbsp olive oil
   1 tbsp salt

naan bread

Naan bread is perfect for mopping up spicy curries or soups. It can also be cooked stuffed with raisins, almonds or thin slices of meat.

ingredients

makes 4 naan breads

1 *300g/10oz/2½ cups self-raising flour, plus extra for dusting*

1 tsp salt

1 tsp baking powder

100g/3½oz live natural yoghurt

90ml/3fl oz/⅓ cup lukewarm water

method

1 Place the flour, salt and baking powder in a mixing bowl and add the yoghurt. Mix well to combine, then cover with a clean cloth and leave for 1 hour in a warm place to rest. Mix in the water and knead for 10 minutes until the dough is smooth. Alternatively, mix in a food processor with a dough hook on a slow speed for 10 minutes. Cover and leave for 1 hour in a warm place to rest.

Turn out the dough on to a well-floured board and divide into 4 balls. Roll out each ball into a circle about 2mm/⅛in thick, cover and leave to rest for 10 minutes in a warm place. Preheat the grill to medium, or heat a frying pan over a medium heat. Cook the breads for 2–3 minutes on each side until golden and puffed up.

asian flat breads

Similar to naan breads, these are slightly lighter, seasoned breads particularly well suited to the flavours of traditional Thai cooking.

method

1 Place the milk, eggs, coriander and garlic in a food processor, and process until smooth.

2 Sift the flour, baking powder and seasoning into a large mixing bowl and stir in half the milk and eggs. Beat for 1 minute, then add almost all the remaining liquid, keeping a little in reserve. Mix well to combine, adding the remaining liquid if the mixture seems dry. Turn out on to a floured board and knead for 10 minutes by hand. Alternatively, mix in a food processor with a dough hook on a slow speed for 10 minutes. Divide the dough in half and wrap in clingfilm. Leave to rest in a warm place for 2 hours.

Preheat the grill to medium. Roll out both pieces of dough until 2mm/⅛in thick and, using a small plate as a guide, cut 2 rounds out of each. Grill the bread rounds for 2–3 minutes on each side until browned and crispy.

ingredients

makes 4 flat breads

1 *90ml/3fl oz/⅓ cup milk*
2 medium eggs
4 sprigs coriander
4 garlic cloves

2 *500g/1lb/4 cups strong white flour,*
plus extra for dusting
½ tsp baking powder
½ tsp salt
½ tsp black pepper

brioche

A rich, buttery bread, brioche tastes best freshly baked, but also toasts wonderfully for pâté or preserves. It is rather time-consuming to prepare, but well worth the effort. Any leftovers can be used in bread and butter pudding (omit the butter, though, as brioche is rich enough) or as breadcrumbs for fish.

ingredients

makes 1 loaf

1 *4 tbsp milk, warmed*
30g/1oz/1½ tbsp fresh yeast,
*   or 1 tbsp dried yeast*
1 tbsp flour
30g/1oz/2 tbsp caster sugar

2 *625g/1¼lb/5 cups unbleached plain*
*   white flour, plus extra for dusting*
1 tsp salt
30g/1oz/2 tbsp caster sugar
4 medium eggs, beaten

3 *275g/9oz/1⅛ cups unsalted butter,*
*   softened*

4 *1 egg yolk beaten with 1 tbsp milk*
*   for glazing*

method

1 Place the warmed milk in a small bowl and whisk in the yeast. Allow to stand for 5 minutes. Stir in the flour and sugar, and set aside for 30 minutes.

2 Place the flour, salt and sugar in a mixing bowl, and make a well in the centre. Pour in the yeasted milk and the eggs. Using your fingers, lightly bring the flour and liquid together, until a dough begins to form, then turn out on to a floured board and knead for 15–20 minutes, until elastic and smooth.

3 Gently beat the softened butter with the back of a spoon until smooth, then add gradually to the dough, about 2 tablespoonfuls at a time. Knead the dough between your fingertips to incorporate the butter, until thoroughly combined. Repeat until all the butter has been added. Leave in a warm place, covered with a clean cloth, for 2 hours or until the dough has doubled in size. Knock it back by either punching it down or turning it over on itself. Cover and rest in the refrigerator for several hours, preferably overnight.

4 Turn out the dough on to a board and shape into a round ball. Cut off one-third and shape into an elongated egg. Roll the remaining dough into a fat sausage and coil around the base of a brioche mould, 23cm/9in in diameter. Leave a hole in the centre of the coil of dough and press the narrower end of the egg-shaped piece of dough inside. Leave in a warm place for 1½–2 hours until doubled in size.
  Preheat the oven to 220°C/425°F/Gas 7. Brush the loaf with the beaten egg and milk, and bake for 40–45 minutes, until golden brown and well risen. Unmould immediately and place on a wire rack to cool.

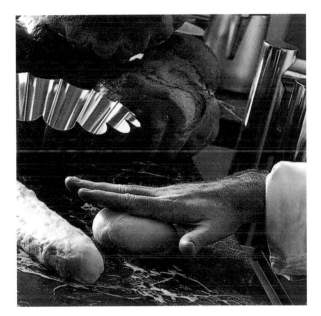

steamed ginger buns

Steamed buns, both stuffed and plain, are a classic element of Chinese cuisine, and accompany savoury and sweet dishes to great effect. Ginger buns are especially good with red curries or Thai pork.

ingredients

makes 12 buns

1 *2 garlic cloves, crushed*
250ml/8fl oz/1 cup warm water
2 tbsp pure sesame oil
2 tbsp ginger juice (page 217)
15g/½oz fresh yeast, or 2 tsp
*   dried yeast*
15g/½oz/1 tbsp caster sugar
425g/14oz/3½ cups plain flour,
*   plus extra for dusting*
125g/4oz/1 cup cornflour
1 tbsp salt

2 *2 tsp corn oil*
125g/4oz root ginger, peeled and
*   finely chopped*
125g/4oz spring onions, finely sliced

method

1 Place the garlic in a blender or food processor with the water, oil and ginger juice. Process until smooth. Transfer to a small bowl and stir in the yeast. Let the mixture stand for 1 minute, then add the sugar, and mix well. Sift the flour and cornflour together 3 times, to ensure they are fully aerated, then stir in the salt. Place in a mixing bowl, add the yeast, and mix gently by hand until a soft dough begins to form. If necessary, add more warm water. Knead for 2 minutes, then transfer to a floured work surface and leave to rest.

2 Warm the oil in a frying pan over a low heat and sweat the ginger until fragrant, about 2–3 minutes. Add the spring onions, toss well, then remove from the heat and allow to cool. Shape the dough into a ball and cut a cross in the centre, pulling back the four corners to make a hole. Place the ginger and spring onions in the hole, and gently pull the sides of the dough up and over to cover. Repeat this process, bringing the dough round and in, thumbs pressing into the centre of the ball, until the spring onions are completely incorporated, about 3–4 minutes.

  Roll the dough into a long sausage, then divide into 12 pieces. Shape into small round balls and set aside in a warm place to prove for 20–30 minutes. Bring some water to the boil in a steamer or pan. Place the buns in the steamer, or in a colander over the pan, cover and steam for 12–15 minutes, until risen and just firm.

assembly

Serve hot with Thai curries or roast meats, or cut in half and stuff with steamed pork or duck.

muffins

Muffins, an American invention, have long been a staple of East Coast breakfasts, and come packed with a variety of fruits and spices to suit individual tastes. Blueberry muffins are a classic, and are made here using fresh or frozen blueberries and topped with flaked almonds.

ingredients

makes 12–15 muffins

1 *150g/5oz/⅔ cup unsalted butter*
200g/7oz/⅞ cup caster sugar
5 medium eggs, separated
250g/8oz/2 cups flaked almonds
250g/8oz/2 cups plain flour
1 tsp baking powder

2 *extra butter and flour for preparing muffin tin*
125g/4oz/1 cup blueberries, or another soft fruit if preferred
30g/1oz/¼ cup flaked almonds

method

1 Cream together the butter and half the sugar in a bowl until soft and pale. Add the egg yolks, stirring gently to combine, and fold in the flaked almonds. Sift the flour and baking powder, and fold into the mixture. Whisk the egg whites with the remaining sugar until they form soft peaks, then gently fold into the batter mixture.

2 Preheat the oven to 180°C/350°F/Gas 4. Grease a muffin tin with butter and dust with flour. Spoon in the mixture to half-fill each mould, and add 1 tablespoonful of blueberries, or other soft fruit. Fill the moulds to the top with the remaining batter, and sprinkle with flaked almonds. Bake for 18–20 minutes until golden, and a skewer or cake tester comes out clean.

assembly

Serve immediately, hot from the oven.

croissants and danish pastries

Croissant and Danish pastry dough is best made the evening before, and allowed to rest overnight. Always use iced water as this prevents the dough becoming warm and sticky. The same dough can also be used to make *pain au raisin* or *pain au chocolat*: simply add dried fruit or sticks of dark chocolate and shape accordingly.

method

1 Dissolve the salt and sugar in one-third of the iced water. Whisk the yeast in the remaining water, and stir in the milk powder. Sift the flour into a large mixing bowl and make a well in the centre. Pour in the sugar and salt mixture, mixing thoroughly, then add the yeast mixture. Mix for 4–5 minutes until well combined. (Alternatively, using a dough hook, mix on a slow speed in a food processor for 4 minutes.) On a floured board, knead the dough for 5 minutes. Place in a greased bowl and leave to rest in a warm place for 6–8 hours, until it has doubled in size.

2 Knock back the dough, turning it over and punching out any air with your fist, then roll it out on a floured board into a rectangle, about 30 x 40cm/12 x 16in. Soften the block of butter by beating it with a rolling pin, then place it in the centre of the rectangle. Fold one of the longer edges of the dough towards the middle, half-covering the butter, and repeat with the other side, so that the butter is under 2 flaps of dough. Fold over the short ends to make a long narrow rectangle. Seal the edges with the rolling pin, wrap in clingfilm and rest in the refrigerator for 1 hour.

Unwrap the dough and place on a cold floured board with the longer edges towards you. Roll out a second time into a rectangle. Repeat the folding, wrap in clingfilm and refrigerate overnight if possible.

(continued overleaf)

ingredients

makes 16 croissants or danish pastries
1 1 tbsp salt
45g/1½oz/3 tbsp caster sugar
300ml/½ pint/1¼ cups iced water
15g/½oz fresh yeast, or 2 tsp dried yeast
20g/¾oz/3 tbsp skimmed milk powder
500g/1lb/4 cups strong white flour, plus extra for dusting

2 200g/7oz/scant 1 cup unsalted butter

(continued overleaf)

croissants and danish pastries (continued)

ingredients

3 croissants
butter for greasing
1 medium egg, beaten

4 danish pastries
butter for greasing
2 tbsp apricot jam, melted
500g/1lb eating apples, peeled, cored and sliced
or 500g/1lb/2½ cups fresh raspberries, blueberries or other fruit
caster sugar for sprinkling

method

3 For croissants, roll out the dough on a floured board into a long rectangle, about 1cm/½in thick. Allow to rest for 5 minutes, then cut the dough in half lengthwise. Cut each of the lengths into 8 triangles and place them on greased baking sheets. Cover the sheet with clingfilm and refrigerate for 5–10 minutes.

   Taking one triangle at a time, lay it on the floured surface, longer point facing you, flat base away, and carefully roll up into a croissant shape, bringing the flat edge towards you. Ensure that the pointed end is in the middle of the finished roll, and place the point face down on the baking sheet, in order to prevent it rising during cooking. Brush the croissant with beaten egg. Repeat with all the triangles. Leave to rise in a warm place for about 1½ hours, until doubled in size.

   Preheat the oven to 230°/450°F/Gas 8. Bake for 15–20 minutes, turning the baking sheets half-way through cooking to ensure an even colour. Remove from the oven and transfer to a wire rack to cool.

4 To make Danish pastries, roll out the dough on a floured board into a long rectangle about 1cm/½in thick. Allow to rest for 5 minutes. Trim the edges of the rectangle and roll up along one long edge to make a long thin roll of dough. Using a sharp knife, cut into slices about 2.5cm/1in wide and place 5cm/2in apart on greased baking sheets. Slightly flatten each roll with the palm of your hand and brush with apricot jam. Leave to rise in a warm place for 1½ hours, until doubled in size.

   Preheat the oven to 230°C/450°F/Gas 8. Dot each slice with apple slices, raspberries or blueberries, and bake for 15–20 minutes, turning the baking sheets half-way through cooking to ensure an even colour. Sprinkle with sugar and return to the oven for 1–2 minutes. Remove from the oven and leave to cool on a wire rack.

assembly

Serve warm, or at room temperature, with extra butter and jam if preferred.

spice and sugar

The true test of any cook's repertoire is their puddings. Perhaps it is because at this point temptation is the key, rather than any more calculated attempt to impress, and there are few gourmets who will not be flattered by a little seduction. However, the long-accepted doctrine of 'the sweeter, the better' is these days becoming rather tired. Yes, chocolate anything will always hit home, but a more subtle way of appealing to the craving for sugar is via its alter ego, spice.

Cinnamon, cardamom, ginger, cloves, nutmeg, vanilla: all are highly intense, inimitable flavours whose value has been recognized throughout the world for centuries. And even today, no store cupboard can consider itself complete without a whole range of spices, enlivening the flavour of so many otherwise ordinary foods: cinnamon for Panettone Bread and Butter Pudding; vanilla for Custard Tart with Armagnac Prunes and also for Caramel Ice-Cream; preserved root ginger to boost Ginger Puddings with Ginger Syrup – the list is endless. Make up a jar of Vanilla Sugar (page 216) and use it as a substitute for caster sugar, and you'll be amazed at the difference. Sugar and spice: what could be nicer?

vanilla pod

steamed sticky rice and banana

Quite different from anything you have ever tasted, this is one of the most popular sweets in Thailand, where it is sold on street corners and eaten with the fingers.

ingredients

serves 4

1 *90g/3oz/⅓ cup black sticky rice*
250g/8oz/1 cup white sticky rice
90g/3oz/⅓ cup caster sugar

2 *2 bananas*
150ml/¼ pint/⅔ cup coconut milk,
homemade (page 10) or canned
60g/2oz/¼ cup caster sugar
½ tsp salt

3 *2 banana leaves*

4 *150g/5oz palm sugar*

method

1 Using separate bowls of cold water, soak the black rice for 3 hours, and the white rice for 1 hour. Drain separately. Line a steamer tray or a colander with a cloth, and place the black rice inside. Sprinkle with 2 tablespoonfuls of sugar. Cover and steam over boiling water for 30–40 minutes until just tender. Repeat with the white rice, sprinkling it with 4 tablespoonfuls of sugar and steaming for 25–30 minutes.

2 Peel and halve the bananas. Place the coconut milk, sugar and salt in a pan and bring to the boil, stirring. Add the bananas and cook for 3 minutes. Remove from the heat. Allow to cool in the milk, then remove with a slotted spoon.

3 Cut 5 x 30cm/12in squares from the 2 banana leaves. Cut one of the squares into 4 smaller pieces, about 15 x 10cm/6 x 4in. Blanch the leaves in boiling water for 20 seconds. Drain and dry with paper towels. Lay one of the larger squares on a flat surface, and place a smaller piece of leaf on the central diagonal. Spread 1 tablespoonful of white rice over the smaller square, leaving a 1cm/½in border all round. Cover with another thin layer of black rice, and place a piece of banana on top. Cover with a layer of black rice, and then a top layer of white rice, and drizzle with 1 tablespoonful of cooking liquid. Take 2 opposite corners of the larger piece of leaf, bring them together and roll them down, one over the other, wrapping the rice tightly inside. Fold the remaining 2 corners over this fold, and turn the parcel over so that all the tucks are underneath. Repeat with the remaining leaves, then steam the parcels for 25 minutes.

4 Gently melt the palm sugar in a small pan, taking care not to let it boil, as this will spoil the flavour.

assembly

Cut the parcels in half just off the diagonal. Rest one half over the other on individual plates. Drizzle with a little of the cooking liquid, and spoon over the melted sugar.

chocolate brownies

Chocolate brownies make a lovely mid-afternoon treat, and are also good dressed up for supper with a little vanilla ice-cream or crème fraîche. Easy and quick to make, they are worth having to hand for any occasion.

method

1 Preheat the oven to 150°C/300°F/Gas 2. Beat together the eggs and sugar until pale. Melt the butter in a pan over a gentle heat and stir in the cocoa, then stir in the egg mixture. Stir in the vanilla, nuts, flour and bourbon or brandy, if using. Pack the mixture into a baking tin measuring 30 x 23cm/12 x 9in, and about 2.5cm/1in deep, and smooth the surface with the back of a spoon. Bake for 20–25 minutes. Allow to cool, then cut into 24 pieces.

assembly

Sift over a little icing sugar, and remove from the tin.

ingredients

makes 24
1 *4 medium eggs*
500g/1lb/2 cups caster sugar
325g/11oz/1⅓ cups unsalted butter
125g/4oz/1 cup cocoa powder
1 tsp vanilla essence
150g/5oz/1 cup roasted hazelnuts
250g/8oz/2 cups plain flour, sifted
2 tsp bourbon or brandy (optional)

to serve
2 tbsp icing sugar

ginger puddings with ginger syrup

Cleverly disguised as an elegant, grown-up dessert, these individual ginger puddings, topped with slices of preserved ginger and a sticky sweet syrup, are nursery food at its very best. Quick to make, they are sure to become a staple treat.

ingredients

serves 8

1 *125g/4oz preserved ginger in syrup*
butter for greasing
caster sugar for coating

2 *300g/10oz/1¼ cups unsalted butter*
300g/10oz/1⅔ cups dark brown
   sugar
1½ tbsp black treacle
2 medium eggs
½ tsp baking powder
2 tsp ground ginger
300g/10oz/2½ cups self-raising
   flour, sifted

to serve

500ml/17fl oz/2 cups custard
   (page 217)

method

1 Finely slice the preserved ginger into 5mm/¼in rounds, reserving the syrup. Grease 8 ramekins or small pudding moulds with a little butter and sprinkle with sugar. Place the ginger slices in the ramekins, drizzle with a little of the reserved syrup to cover the base, and set aside.

2 Preheat the oven to 180°C/350°F/Gas 4. Cream the butter and sugar in a mixing bowl until smooth, then add the treacle. Stir in the eggs one at a time, add the baking powder, ground ginger and flour, and mix well. Divide the mixture between the sugared ramekins, and place them in a large baking tin, then pour in enough warm water to come half-way up the sides of the ramekins (if using metal containers for the puddings, line the tin with a tea towel to prevent the metal becoming too hot). Bake for 40 minutes, or until the puddings are firm to the touch. Remove from the oven and leave for 10–15 minutes to settle. If preferred, the puddings can be made in advance and then reheated later in a medium oven.

assembly

Gently press the edges of the puddings with your fingertips, bringing the sides away from the tins, and turn out on to individual plates. Serve with custard.

lemon and mascarpone layer cake

Don't worry if the meringue discs in this recipe break when you remove them from the baking sheet: the layers of mascarpone and lemon curd will stick them together again once the cake is assembled. Any surplus lemon curd can be stored in the fridge for up to a month. If pushed, you can buy ready-made, but the two are worlds apart taste-wise.

method

1 Preheat the oven to 120°C/250°F/Gas ½. Beat the egg whites until they begin to stand in peaks, then add the sugar a little at a time, whisking until stiff. Line 2 baking sheets with greaseproof paper and butter well. Using a medium nozzle, pipe one-third of the meringue mixture on to the 2 baking sheets in a continuous snail-shell formation until about 15cm/6in in diameter. Alternatively, spoon the mixture on to the sheets, and spread with the flat of a knife into rounds. Repeat twice, or until you have 6 meringue discs. Bake for 35–40 minutes, or until the centre is firm to the touch. Allow to cool. To remove the paper, wipe with a damp cloth, leave for 1 minute, then peel off.

2 To make the lemon curd, grate the zest from 2 of the lemons and squeeze the juice of all 3. Set aside half the zest with 2 tablespoonfuls of lemon juice, and place the remainder in the base of a glass or enamel mixing bowl. Add the beaten eggs, then stir in half the sugar. Bring a pan of water to the boil and place the bowl over the top. Add the butter and cook for about 20 minutes, stirring frequently, until the mixture starts to thicken. Remove from the heat and allow to cool.

3 Mix the mascarpone with the double cream, the remaining lemon zest, juice and sugar. Place 1 meringue disc on a cake plate. Smooth on a layer of mascarpone, and then a thin layer of the lemon curd, and top with another meringue disc. Repeat the layers until all the ingredients are used; the final meringue disc should form the top of the cake.

assembly

Dust with a little icing sugar and cut into thin wedges.

ingredients

serves 8

1 meringue
8 medium egg whites
300g/10oz/1¼ cups vanilla sugar (page 216)
butter for greasing

2 lemon curd
3 lemons
2 medium eggs, beaten
175g/6oz/¾ cup caster sugar
60g/2oz/¼ cup unsalted butter, cut into small chunks

3 *375g/12oz/1½ cups mascarpone*
100ml/3½fl oz/generous ⅓ cup double cream

to serve
a little icing sugar

caramelized pear and polenta tart

Combining poached pears and an unusual polenta pastry, this sweet tart makes a light, delicate summer pudding. It is equally good for breakfast with fresh coffee.

ingredients

serves 4

1 375g/12oz/3 cups plain flour
pinch of salt
125g/4oz/½ cup caster sugar
125g/4oz/½ cup polenta
200g/7oz/scant 1 cup unsalted
    butter, cut into 7 or 8 small pieces
1 medium egg
1 medium egg yolk

2 325g/11oz/1⅓ cups caster sugar
250g/8oz/1 cup soft demerara
    sugar
1 litre/1¾ pints/4 cups water
60ml/2fl oz/¼ cup white wine
1 vanilla pod, sliced down the centre
    and beans removed
rind of half a lemon
juice of 1 lemon
1 cinnamon stick
6 firm pears, peeled
butter, for greasing

to serve

60ml/2fl oz/¼ cup Jersey or
    double cream

method

1 Sift the flour into a large bowl and add the salt, sugar and polenta. Mix well. Add the butter, and mix into the flour using a blunt knife, until the mixture resembles fine breadcrumbs. (This takes a little longer than the conventional rubbing-in with fingertips, but will result in a better pastry.) Combine the egg and egg yolk with a fork, add to the bowl, and knead the dough until it forms a soft, pliable ball. Wrap in clingfilm and refrigerate for 2 hours.

2 Place 250g/8oz/1 cup of the caster sugar in a large pan and add the demerara sugar, water, white wine, vanilla pod, lemon rind and juice and the cinnamon stick. Bring to the boil and simmer until the sugar is dissolved. Add the pears and reduce the heat. Cover and cook for 20 minutes, then remove from the heat and leave to cool in the pan, about 2 hours. Remove the pears and reserve. Place the pan over a high heat and simmer until the syrup has reduced by two-thirds. Strain and set aside.

   Preheat the oven to 180°C/350°F/Gas 4. Roll out the chilled dough into a round about 5mm/¼in thick and use to line a lightly greased ceramic tart case, about 23cm/9in in diameter. Press well into the sides and trim, leaving a slight overhang to allow for shrinkage. Remove the cores from the cooled pears and slice into quarters. Arrange the pears in the pastry case and sprinkle with the remaining caster sugar. Bake for 45 minutes, until the pastry is lightly golden. Remove and allow to cool for 15 minutes.

assembly

Cut the tart into wedges and serve with the reduced syrup and spoonfuls of cream.

caramelized sago pudding with coconut milk

A wonderful variation on that childhood nightmare, sago pudding, this version is scented with coconut and set in small moulds over caramel, to give it a texture and sweetness that is a million miles away from school dinners.

method

1 Place the caster sugar and water in a large pan and bring to the boil over a medium heat. Cook until the sugar is dissolved and bubbling and the mixture has turned a caramel colour. Pour into 4 small moulds or ramekins and leave to set for 20 minutes.

2 Rinse the sago under cold running water, then place in a bowl with enough warm water to cover and leave to soak for 1 hour. Place the sugar, salt, coconut milk, water and drained sago in a small pan, and cook over a low heat, stirring constantly, until the mixture has thickened, about 10 minutes. Do not allow to boil. Pour into the caramel-lined moulds and leave to set for 3 hours.

3 Using two separate pans, gently heat the palm sugar and coconut cream until just melted. Do not allow to brown.

assembly

Dip the moulds in hot water to loosen the caramel, and turn out on to 4 plates. Pour over the melted palm sugar and drizzle with the coconut cream.

ingredients

serves 4

1 *90g/3oz/⅓ cup caster sugar*
4 tbsp water

2 *90g/3oz/½ cup sago*
300g/10oz/1¼ cups caster sugar
pinch of salt
500ml/17fl oz/2¼ cups coconut milk, homemade (page 10) or canned
350ml/12fl oz/1½ cups water

3 *60g/2oz palm sugar*
60g/2oz coconut cream (page 10)

plum or fig *tartes fines*

These fine pastry rounds can be decorated with any number of fruits, but are especially good with plums or figs. Always taste the fruit first to measure its sweetness, adding extra sugar for particularly sharp fruit. Ideally, however, buy the best quality fruit in season and it will be sweet enough.

method

1 On a floured surface, roll out the puff pastry very thinly, about 2.5mm/⅛in thick. Place a small plate, 15cm/6in in diameter, on top of the pastry and cut round it with a sharp knife to make 4 pastry circles. Place on a lightly greased baking sheet and prick thoroughly with a fork, leaving a 1cm/½in margin untouched so that it will puff up when cooked. Leave to rest in the refrigerator for 30 minutes.

2 Preheat the oven to 180°C/350°F/Gas 4. Cut the fruit in half top to bottom and, if using plums, remove the stones. Thinly slice the halves into smaller pieces, about 2.5mm/⅛in thick. Sprinkle the pastry with a little of the sugar and lay the fruit in concentric circles, beginning 1cm/½in from the outside edge and working inwards. Place in the oven for 20–25 minutes, until the pastry has begun to brown. Sprinkle with the remaining sugar and return to the oven for a further 2 minutes.

assembly

Serve warm or at room temperature with crème fraîche or ice-cream.

ingredients

serves 4

1 *flour for dusting*
1kg/2lb puff pastry (page 214)
butter for greasing

2 *500g/1lb ripe plums or figs*
60g/2oz/¼ cup caster sugar

to serve
*200ml/7fl oz/scant 1 cup crème
fraîche or ice-cream*

champagne and summer fruit jelly

Packed with the colours and taste of summer, this is the adult version of jelly and ice-cream. If you can stretch to pink Champagne, it is worth it for the colour and the flavour. Always use the best gelatine you can buy as the quality is directly related to the success of the set.

ingredients

serves 4

1 *1 bottle Champagne, preferably pink*
400g/13oz/1⅔ cups caster sugar
1 vanilla bean
250g/8oz cherries, pitted

2 *1 litre/1¾ pints/4 cups warm water*
7 leaves gelatine, preferably gold leaf (page 11)

3 *250g/8oz/1½ cups raspberries*
250g/8oz/1½ cups blueberries
250g/8oz/1½ cups strawberries, halved

to serve

250ml/8fl oz/1 cup crème fraîche

method

1 Measure 200ml/7fl oz/scant 1 cup Champagne into a pan. Add the sugar and vanilla bean, and bring to the boil over a medium heat, stirring until all the sugar dissolves. Add the cherries and simmer for 2–3 minutes until the fruit begins to bleed (be careful not to overcook as this will spoil the flavour). Remove from the heat, drain and set aside.

2 Pour the warm water into a bowl and add the gelatine. Leave for 5 minutes until softened and transparent, then remove with a slotted spoon and discard the water. Take a small cupful of the cherry liquid and cool to body temperature (test with your little finger) with some of the remaining Champagne. Add the gelatine, stir until dissolved, and return the mixture to the rest of the cherry liquid. Add the remaining Champagne and allow to cool for 5–10 minutes.

3 Discard the vanilla bean and pour half the cherry liquid into the base of a 600ml/1 pint/2½ cup jelly mould (or moulds, if you are making individual jellies). Add half the raspberries, blueberries and strawberries, packing tight and making sure the fruit is evenly distributed, and leave in the refrigerator for about 1 hour to set. Once it is firm, fill to the top with the remaining fruit and cherry liquid, and chill once again until the jelly has set.

If you fail to achieve a set after the first chilling, return the fruit and liquid to the pan and add 2 extra leaves of gelatine, dissolving them in a little warm water first, before returning to the mould and chilling once more.

assembly

Dip the mould briefly in hot water, then turn out the jelly on to a large platter (or plates, if jellies are individual) and serve with crème fraîche.

vanilla custard tart with armagnac prunes

Light and eggy, with prunes heavily doused in Armagnac, this dessert is perfect for Christmas-time suppers, when you crave something delicate that still has a festive kick. Be sure to give the prunes their full soaking time, as this is essential for both texture and flavour.

ingredients

serves 4

1 *1.3 litres/2¼ pints/5⅔ cups water*
2 Darjeeling tea-bags
250g/8oz/1 cup caster sugar
rind and juice of ½ orange
rind and juice of 1 lemon
1kg/2lb pitted prunes
250ml/8fl oz/1 cup Armagnac

2 *sweet shortcrust pastry (page 216)*
flour for dusting
butter for greasing

3 custard
900ml/1½ pints/3½ cups double
  cream
3 medium eggs
175g/6oz/¾ cup vanilla sugar
  (page 216)
75g/2½oz/5 tbsp unsalted butter,
  diced
4 tbsp Armagnac

method

1 Place the water, tea-bags, sugar, orange rind and juice, and lemon rind and juice in a pan and bring to a rolling boil. Add the prunes, then remove from the heat and leave to cool in the liquid. When they are cold, pour over the Armagnac and leave for 48 hours to steep.

2 Preheat the oven to 180°C/350°F/Gas 4. Roll out the pastry into a round on a lightly floured surface and use to line a 23cm/9in greased, loose-bottomed flan tin. Rest the pastry for 30 minutes in the refrigerator, then line with greaseproof paper, fill with baking beans, and bake blind for 15 minutes. Remove the beans and paper and bake for a further 5 minutes, or until the pastry is dry and just beginning to colour. Leave the tin on a wire rack to cool. Keep the oven at the same temperature.

3 Mix together the cream, eggs, vanilla sugar, butter and Armagnac in a bowl, and pour into the prepared pastry case. Bake for 35–40 minutes, or until just cooked (the centre should still be slightly soft). Leave the flan to cool on a wire rack for at least 30 minutes, to allow it to set before removing from the tin.

assembly

Once cool, cut the tart into large wedges and serve with the prunes to one side.

white chocolate mousse with blackberries

This wonderful late-summer pudding can be adapted for all seasons simply by changing the fruit: preserved cherries or figs for winter, strawberries for late spring. It is quite rich, so keep portions small, and always give it the full refrigeration time, or you'll be left with a rather runny, albeit delicious, mess.

method

1 Preheat the oven to 200°C/400°F/Gas 6. Place the flour, ground and flaked hazelnuts and sugar in a mixing bowl and rub in half the butter. Add the egg yolk and gather the mixture together into a ball. Roll out the pastry on a lightly floured surface into a round approximately 5mm/¼in thick. Grease a 25cm/10in loose-bottomed or springform flan tin and cut out the pastry to fit the base. Press down well, line with greaseproof paper, fill with baking beans, and bake blind for 15 minutes. Remove the paper and beans, return the pastry to the oven for 5 minutes, then leave to cool on a wire rack, still in the tin.

2 Whisk the egg yolks in a food processor on slow speed until pale and tripled in volume, 6–8 minutes. Fold half the melted chocolate into the egg yolks. Gently melt the butter, mixing in the remaining chocolate and fold into the eggs. Whisk the egg whites with the sugar until they form soft peaks, and fold into the chocolate mixture. Make sure the chocolate does not cool before the egg whites are added, or the mixture will separate. Gently stir in the whipped cream. Line the cooled pastry base with half the blackberries, then pour over the chocolate mousse. Refrigerate for 3 hours.

assembly

Remove the mousse from the tin, cut into wedges, and place in the centre of individual serving plates. Circle with the remaining blackberries, and serve.

ingredients

serves 8–10

1 175g/6oz/1¼ cups plain flour,
     plus extra for dusting
   2 tbsp ground hazelnuts
   2 tsp flaked hazelnuts
   45g/1½oz/3 tbsp caster sugar
   300g/10oz/1¼ cups unsalted butter,
     plus extra for greasing
   1 medium egg yolk

2 5 medium egg yolks
   425g/14oz/14 squares white
     chocolate, melted (page 221)
   150g/5oz/⅔ cup unsalted butter
   4 medium egg whites
   150g/5oz/⅔ cup caster sugar
   250ml/8fl oz/1 cup whipping
     cream, whipped
   250g/8oz/2 cups blackberries,
     washed and drained

orange crème renversée

A welcome alternative to crème caramel, these custards are easy to make, and require no last-minute preparation other than turning out. Ideally, make them in the morning to be eaten the same day, as they will not keep longer than 36 hours, and always allow the full chilling time, since this will affect both flavour and consistency.

ingredients

serves 4

1 *5 medium egg yolks*
1 medium egg
90g/3oz/⅓ cup caster sugar
400ml/14fl oz/1¾ cups double cream
200ml/7fl oz/scant 1 cup full-fat milk
1 tsp grated orange zest

2 *90g/3oz/⅓ cup caster sugar*
2 tsp water

method

1 Gently mix together the egg yolks, egg and sugar. Bring the cream, milk and orange zest just to the boil in a large pan, then remove from the heat and allow to cool for 10 minutes. Pour the scalded cream mixture over the eggs and sugar, and stir lightly with a wooden spoon, creating as few bubbles as possible, as too much air in the mixture will spoil the consistency of the puddings. Skim off any foam and set aside.

2 Preheat the oven to 150°C/300°F/Gas 2. (Ideally, do not use a fan-assisted oven, as the vibrations will whip up too much air.) Make a caramel by gently melting the sugar in a shallow pan over a low heat until it begins to darken in colour and is quite liquid. Remove from the heat and stir in the water, taking care, because the sugar will spit. Pour into the bottom of 4 individual pudding moulds, and allow to cool. When the caramel has set, about 5 minutes, fill with the orange custard. Place the moulds in a roasting tin and pour in enough warm water to come half-way up the sides (if using metal moulds, place a cloth in the bottom of the roasting tin, to prevent too intense a heat). Bake for 40–45 minutes, or until just set but not browned. Remove from the oven and allow to cool, then chill in the refrigerator for about 8 hours.

assembly

When ready to serve, gently press your finger around the edges of the custard, easing it away from the sides (it may be necessary to run a knife round the edge). Turn each mould upside-down on a serving plate, and allow the custard to slide out. Drizzle with any remaining caramel in the base of the mould.

panettone bread and butter pudding

The old favourites are always the best, and bread and butter pudding is no exception. There is no better future for leftover panettone than this warm, creamy dessert, spiced with vanilla and cinnamon. However, this recipe works equally well with any kind of bread, from ordinary white to croissants, brioche or *pain au chocolat*.

ingredients

serves 4

1 *700ml/1¼ pints/3 cups double cream*
700ml/1¼ pints/3 cups milk
1 vanilla pod
4 medium eggs
3 medium egg yolks
125g/4oz/½ cup caster sugar

2 *30g/1oz/2 tbsp unsalted butter*
2 tbsp sugar
½ medium-sized panettone (or similar Italian sweet fruit bread)
4 cinnamon sticks

to serve
crème fraîche

method

1 Mix the cream and milk in a bowl. Split the vanilla pod lengthwise and scrape out the seeds with a teaspoon. Add the seeds to the milk and stir well (reserve the pod for making vanilla sugar, page 216). Whisk the eggs, egg yolks and sugar in a large bowl. Add the milk and cream, and blend with a fork (do not whisk as this will put too much air into the custard).

2 Preheat the oven to 160°C/325°F/Gas 3. Grease a 30 x 20cm/12 x 8in baking tin or dish with butter, and sprinkle with sugar to coat. Cut the panettone into large hunks about 2cm/¾in thick and lay them across the bottom of the dish. Pour over the custard and dot with the remaining butter. Push the cinnamon sticks into the custard, so that they are covered but not hidden, and sprinkle with the remaining sugar. Leave to rest for at least 10 minutes to allow the bread to absorb the custard, then bake for 35–40 minutes. The pudding is ready when the surface is just turning golden and the custard is almost set. Remove from the oven and allow to rest for 15–20 minutes – the custard will then finish cooking and set firm.

assembly

Remove the cinnamon sticks and serve at room temperature, cut into generous squares and accompanied by a little crème fraîche.

lemon balm ice-cream

This is a refreshing, summery dessert that is a perfect foil for spicy Thai curries or fish. Lemon balm grows easily in the garden or in window-boxes, and has a wonderful scent in midsummer, so it is worth cultivating. Beware, however, as it is incredibly prolific – if you value potting space, stick to buying it ready picked from the supermarket.

method

1 If time allows, place the milk and cream in a bowl with the lemon balm, slightly crushed to release the flavour, and leave in the refrigerator overnight to infuse.

2 Place the lemon balm mixture in a pan and bring to the boil. Whisk together the egg yolks and sugar in a bowl. Pour in half the boiling milk, then return the mixture to the pan. Lower the heat and simmer until the mixture begins to thicken, 5–6 minutes, stirring constantly with a wooden spoon and scraping the bottom. Do not allow it to boil. Remove from the heat and pass through a fine conical sieve to remove any cooked egg or pieces of lemon balm. Stir in the yoghurt and leave to cool. Churn in an ice-cream maker according to the manufacturer's instructions. Alternatively, place in a plastic bowl in the freezer and chill for about 6 hours, stirring every hour or so, or until the ice-cream is set.

assembly

Remove from the freezer 3–4 minutes before serving to allow the ice-cream to soften. Scoop into balls and decorate with lemon balm leaves.

ingredients

serves 4

1 *475ml/16fl oz/2 cups full-cream milk*
350ml/12 fl oz/1½ cups double
*   cream*
4 sprigs fresh lemon balm

2 *10 medium egg yolks*
300g/10oz/1¼ cups caster sugar
600ml/1 pint/2½ cups natural
*   yoghurt*

to serve
lemon balm leaves

caramel ice-cream

Creamy and sweet, this is really more a parfait than an ice-cream and can be served in a single piece, to be cut into slices at the table and accompanied by fruit and biscuits.

ingredients

serves 4

1 *6 medium egg yolks*
2 tsp water
175g/6oz/¾ cup vanilla sugar
(page 216)
575ml/18fl oz/2⅓ cups double
cream

to serve

8 palmiers, or similar biscuits
200g/7oz/1⅓ cups fresh
raspberries

method

1 Pour boiling water into a mixing bowl and leave for 2 minutes to warm the bowl. Pour off the water, dry the bowl and add the egg yolks (warming the bowl before beating the eggs creates a lighter ice-cream). Beat using a balloon whisk, or an electric mixer set at the highest speed, until airy and smooth. Place the water and sugar in a small pan over a low heat until the sugar has dissolved. Continue to simmer until the sugar darkens and turns to a dark caramel. Slowly pour the caramel over the beaten yolks and whisk vigorously, until the mixture is amalgamated. Using a wooden spoon, fold a quarter of the mixture into the cream, ensuring it is well combined, then fold in the remainder. Pour the mixture into a 600ml/1pint/2½ cup terrine tin or jelly mould lined with clingfilm, and freeze for 6–8 hours until set.

assembly

Turn the ice-cream out of the mould and cut into thick slices or wedges. Serve with palmiers and fresh raspberries.

frozen chocolate and pistachio parfait

In this sumptuous ice-cream cake the sharpness of pistachio is used to cut the richness of the chocolate. Making the two different types of ice-cream may seem labour intensive, but the result is well worth the effort.

ingredients

serves 8–10

1 chocolate ice-cream

8 medium egg yolks
250g/8oz/1 cup caster sugar
500ml/17fl oz/generous 2 cups milk
300ml/½ pint/1¼ cups double cream
250g/8oz/8 squares dark chocolate, broken up (the higher the percentage of cocoa solids the better)

2 pistachio ice-cream

8 medium egg yolks
200g/7oz/scant 1 cup caster sugar
45g/1½oz pistachio paste
500ml/17fl oz/generous 2 cups milk
300ml/½ pint/1¼ cups double cream
60g/2oz chopped pistachio nuts

method

1 First make the chocolate ice-cream: whisk together the egg yolks and sugar in a small bowl. In a small pan, bring the milk and cream to the boil and add the chocolate. Return to the boil, then remove from the heat and stir well to ensure the chocolate is thoroughly melted. Add a little of this mixture to the bowl with the beaten egg yolks and mix well, then pour the egg mixture into the pan of chocolate milk and stir over a low heat for 1–2 minutes. Do not allow to boil. Pass through a conical sieve to remove any cooked egg and leave to cool. Refrigerate when cold.

2 To make the pistachio ice-cream, beat the egg yolks and sugar together until pale, then add the pistachio paste. Bring the milk and cream to the boil, remove from the heat, and stir in the egg mixture. Pass through a conical sieve, then stir in the chopped pistachio nuts, and allow to cool. When the ice-cream is cold, pour half the chocolate ice-cream into the base of a terrine tin or mould, about 30 x 10cm/12 x 4in. Spoon the pistachio ice-cream on top, and finish with the remaining chocolate ice-cream. Place in the freezer overnight to set.

assembly

Turn out on to a large plate and serve in thick slices.

strawberry tortoni

Signor Tortoni was an Italian living in Paris at the end of the eighteenth century. His café was the first to serve this concoction of fruit and cream, later to become known as ice-cream. As good now as it was then, it is easy to make and can be used in the same proportions for virtually any berry or fruit.

method

1 Crush the berries in a shallow dish with the back of a spoon, add the biscuits and the liqueur and leave to macerate for 1 hour. Add the almonds and stir well to break up the biscuits. Add half the sugar. Whip the egg whites and remaining sugar until stiff, and fold half this mixture into the strawberries. Mix in the double cream until well combined, then fold in the remaining egg-white mixture. Spoon into a 600ml/1 pint/2½ cup mould or pudding bowl lined with clingfilm and freeze for 12 hours.

assembly

Remove from the freezer a few minutes before serving and cut into slices or wedges. Serve with extra cream if liked.

ingredients

serves 4
1 *375g/12oz/3 cups strawberries, wiped clean and hulled*
6 amaretti biscuits
125ml/4fl oz/½ cup strawberry liqueur
125g/4oz/1 cup flaked almonds
20g/¾oz/4 tsp caster sugar
3 medium egg whites
475ml/16fl oz/2 cups double cream

to serve
double cream (optional)

champagne and raspberry granita

Light and refreshing, this is ideal for serving between courses, and also makes the perfect conclusion to a heavy meal. It takes no time to prepare, so it's an indulgence you can enjoy without much effort.

method

1 Mix all the ingredients in a bowl, pressing down well in order to crush the raspberries slightly. Transfer to a large dish 3cm/1½in deep and freeze for a minimum of 8 hours, preferably overnight.

assembly

Transfer the granita to individual bowls or glasses and then serve immediately.

ingredients

serves 4
1 *250ml/8fl oz/1 cup Champagne*
250g/8oz/2 cups raspberries, rinsed and drained
4 tsp lemon juice

staple recipes
and glossary of techniques

At Mezzo, the contents of a well-stocked store cupboard provide the basis for many of the recipes. From red curry paste and chilli jam to stocks and sauces, such staples are integral to a wide variety of dishes and allow for constant innovation and reworking of ingredients. Made using the freshest produce and straightforward techniques, they can be prepared in bulk and kept refrigerated, often for up to three months, allowing you to whip up dishes in a fraction of the time normally required – and at a fraction of the price of shop-bought alternatives.

The prospect of making your own sauces, pastries or stocks may seem daunting but, more often than not, this is the easiest part of any recipe, and by far the most satisfying. Five minutes of your time to throw a bunch of ingredients into a food mixer to make a curry paste; two hours' unattended simmering for a handful of beef bones and a couple of vegetables when making a pot of stock; a blitz in a mixer and a rest in the fridge for the best shortcrust pastry: what could be easier? There really is no excuse for spending a small fortune buying less flavourful, preservative-heavy alternatives at the supermarket. So don't be afraid of this chapter: use it and cross-reference it. When you see all those jars of pastes, sauces and jams lined up in your fridge, you'll feel such a sense of smugness, you'll never eat pre-prepared again.

sweet pepper and chilli pepper

chicken stock

makes about 2 litres/3½ pints/8 cups
1kg/2lb chicken carcass and bones, skin removed
60g/2oz leeks, chopped
60g/2oz onion, chopped
60g/2oz celery, chopped
1 bouquet garni

method

Place the chicken carcass and bones in a large pan with enough cold water to cover. Bring to the boil, then skim, and add more cold water to bring the fat to the surface. Skim a second time, and add the vegetables and bouquet garni. Simmer for 3 hours over a low heat, then pass through a fine conical sieve or a muslin-lined colander. Allow to cool, then refrigerate. Skim off any remaining fat. The stock can be kept in the freezer for up to 3 months.

beef stock

makes about 2 litres/3½ pints/8 cups
1kg/2lb beef bones and trimmings
3 litres/5¼ pints/12 cups cold water
2 leeks, roughly chopped
1 onion, halved
3 sticks celery, roughly chopped
2 carrots, chopped
4 garlic cloves
6 black peppercorns
1 bouquet garni

method

Place the beef bones and trimmings in a large pan and cover with most of the cold water. Bring to the boil, skim, and add the remaining water to bring the fat to the surface. Skim again, then add the vegetables, garlic, peppercorns and bouquet garni. Simmer for 3 hours over a low heat, then strain through a fine conical sieve or a colander lined with muslin. The stock can be kept in the freezer for up to 3 months.

red wine jus

A good staple sauce to serve with liver or sweetbreads.

makes 1 litre/1¾ pints/4 cups
750g/1½lb beef bones and trimmings
750g/1½lb veal bones and trimmings
250g/8oz chicken bones and trimmings
1 bulb garlic, divided into cloves
2 carrots, roughly chopped
5 shallots, roughly chopped
3 sticks celery, roughly chopped
1 leek, roughly chopped
250ml/8fl oz/1 cup red wine
2 litres/3½ pints/8 cups water
2 bay leaves
4 sprigs thyme
1 tbsp red wine vinegar
freshly ground black pepper

method

Place the bones and trimmings in a large dry pan with the garlic, and toss over a medium heat until coloured. Add the carrots, followed by the shallots, celery and leek, cover and sweat for 4–5 minutes until the vegetables begin to soften. Add the red wine and simmer for 10 minutes. Pour over the water and bring to the boil. Add the bay leaves and the thyme, reduce the heat and simmer, skimming frequently, for about 3 hours. Add the red wine vinegar, season with black pepper, and strain through a fine conical sieve or a colander lined with muslin.

fish stock

makes about 2 litres/3½ pints/8 cups

1.5kg/3lb fish bones, preferably sole,
*   turbot or whiting*
125g/4oz onions, diced
125g/4oz celery, diced
125g/4oz leeks, diced
1 bouquet garni
200ml/7fl oz/scant 1 cup white wine

method

Wash the fish bones thoroughly under cold running water. Chop roughly and place in a large pan with the vegetables, bouquet garni and white wine. Add enough water to cover, and bring to the boil over a medium heat. Simmer for 20 minutes, skimming frequently, then pass through a fine conical sieve or a colander lined with muslin. Allow to cool, then refrigerate. The stock can be kept in the freezer for up to 3 months.

court bouillon

makes 1.5 litres/2½ pints/6¼ cups

2 leeks, chopped
1 large carrot, chopped
3 sticks celery, chopped
1 medium onion, roughly sliced
2 shallots, chopped
½ fennel bulb, chopped
4 sprigs thyme
4 sprigs tarragon
4 sprigs parsley
2 garlic cloves
1.5 litres/2½ pints/6¼ cups water
1 tsp sea salt
1 tsp black peppercorns
½ lemon
2 star anise
200ml/7fl oz/scant 1 cup dry white wine

method

Place the vegetables, herbs, garlic and water in a large pan, and bring to the boil. Add the salt, pepper, lemon, star anise and white wine, and simmer over a medium heat for 35 minutes. Pass through a conical sieve or in a colander lined with muslin.

vegetable stock

makes about 2 litres/3½ pints/8 cups

2 tbsp olive oil
2 garlic cloves, crushed
1 onion, cut into chunks
1 leek, sliced
½ fennel bulb, sliced
1 stick celery, cut into chunks
1 carrot, cut into chunks
¼ white cabbage, cut into 2.5cm/1in chunks
1 tbsp chopped parsley
1 tbsp chopped chives
2 tbsp chopped basil
1 star anise
10 crushed black peppercorns
pinch of salt

method

Heat the oil in a large pan over a low heat, then add the garlic and all the vegetables except the cabbage, cover and sweat until soft. Add enough water to cover, together with the cabbage, herbs and flavourings, and bring to the boil. Cook for 10 minutes, skimming constantly, then remove from the heat and allow to cool. Pass through a conical sieve or a colander lined with muslin, squeezing out all the juices with the back of a wooden spoon. The stock should be pale in colour and reasonably clear. Allow to cool, then store, covered, in the refrigerator. The stock can be kept in the freezer for up to 3 months.

rouille

Serve with soups, shellfish and bouillabaisse.

makes 300ml/½ pint/1¼ cups
1 garlic clove
½ red chilli, deseeded and roughly chopped
1 egg yolk
small pinch saffron
60g/2oz new potatoes, boiled and drained
200ml/7fl oz/scant 1 cup olive oil
sea salt
freshly ground black pepper

method

Place the garlic, chilli, egg yolk and saffron in the bowl of a food processor, and process to a rough paste. Add the potatoes and process until mixed thoroughly. On a medium speed, slowly add the olive oil until the mixture is thick and smooth. Season to taste and store in an airtight container in the refrigerator. Keeps for up to 1 month.

aïoli

Serve with fish and vegetable dishes.

makes 300ml/½ pint/1¼ cups
1 garlic clove, crushed
2 medium egg yolks
300ml/½ pint/1¼ cups olive oil
sea salt
freshly ground black pepper
1 tbsp lemon juice

method

Place the garlic and egg yolks in a mixing bowl. Gently whisk in the olive oil, pouring in a steady stream. Season with salt and pepper, and add the lemon juice. If the mixture seems a little thick, add a teaspoonful of boiling water. The aïoli will keep, covered, in the refrigerator for up to 3 days.

hollandaise

A good accompaniment to fish and vegetables, especially asparagus.

makes about 200ml/7fl oz/scant 1 cup
1 French shallot, diced
1 garlic clove, finely chopped
pinch of cracked black pepper
pinch of salt
125ml/4fl oz/½ cup white wine vinegar
125ml/4fl oz/½ cup dry white wine
1 sprig tarragon
300g/10oz/1¼ cups butter
2 medium egg yolks

method

Place the shallot, garlic, pepper, salt, vinegar, wine and tarragon in a pan, and bring to the boil. Simmer over a medium heat until reduced by half, then strain through a fine sieve or a colander lined with fine muslin.

Melt the butter in a small pan, then remove from the heat and leave to stand to allow it to clarify. Mix the egg yolks in a heatproof bowl with 3 tablespoonfuls of the liquid. Place over a pan of boiling water and whisk constantly until the eggs are pale and doubled in volume. Remove from the heat. Slowly whisk in the clarified butter, discarding the white scum which will have sunk to the bottom. Keep whisking until you have an emulsified sauce. If it starts to become too thick, add a little boiling water. Taste for seasoning. If necessary, hollandaise can be kept warm in a bain-marie for a short time.

chilli jam

Used in Thai recipes such as stir-fries, meat and vegetable dishes, to give an extra 'kick'.

makes 500ml/17fl oz/generous 2 cups
1 litre/1¾ pints/4 cups sunflower oil
500g/1lb red shallots, sliced lengthwise
250g/8oz garlic cloves, sliced lengthwise
10 large red chillies, deseeded and chopped
100g/3½oz dried shrimps, rinsed and dried
250g/8oz palm sugar
125ml/4fl oz/½ cup thick tamarind water
   (page 217)
1 tsp salt
2 tbsp fish sauce

method

Heat the oil in a wok or deep pan until shimmering, and deep-fry the shallots. (If the oil is too hot they will simply burn rather than gently caramelize.) Cook until crispy and coloured, then remove with a slotted spoon and drain on paper towels. Add the garlic to the hot oil and again cook until crispy and coloured, then remove and drain. Repeat with the chillies, and set aside to drain.

   Place the dried shrimps, palm sugar, tamarind water, salt and fish sauce in the bowl of a food processor. Add the deep-fried shallots, garlic and chillies together with half the oil from the wok, and process until smooth. Transfer to an airtight jar and store in the refrigerator once opened. The jam will keep for up to 3 months.

chilli paste

Use this to make Thai curries.

makes 400ml/14fl oz/1¾ cups
20 dried red chillies, cut in half, deseeded, soaked
   for 30 minutes and drained
8 lime leaves, cut into fine julienne strips
4 stalks lemon grass, peeled and chopped
125g/4oz galangal, peeled and sliced
60g/2oz coriander roots
zest of 6 kaffir limes
60g/2oz Thai shallots, sliced
60g/2oz garlic cloves, sliced
2 tbsp shrimp paste
½ tsp coriander seeds
¼ tsp cumin seeds
small piece mace
5 white peppercorns

method

Preheat the oven to 180°C/350°F/Gas 4. Place the chillies, lime leaves, lemon grass, galangal, coriander roots, lime zest, shallots and garlic in the bowl of a food processor, and process to a thick paste. Alternatively, use a mortar and pestle to pound to a paste. Add the shrimp paste, and process until smooth, adding a little water if the paste is too dry. Place the coriander, cumin and mace on a baking sheet, and roast in the oven for 4–5 minutes until fragrant. Add the peppercorns and remove from the heat. Place in a mortar, or a coffee grinder, and grind finely. Mix the ground spices into the paste. Store in an airtight container for up to 6 months.

red curry paste

The basis of Thai red curries, this paste is particularly good with duck or pork.

makes 500ml/17fl oz/generous 2 cups
10 fresh red chillies, deseeded and chopped
4 stalks lemon grass, peeled and chopped
30g/1oz galangal, peeled and chopped
15 shallots, chopped
10 garlic cloves, chopped
zest of 4 limes, preferably kaffir, chopped
5g/¼oz white peppercorns
20g/¾oz shrimp paste
5g/¼oz roasted dried shrimps

method

Place all the ingredients in the bowl of a food processor and process to a fine paste. Alternatively, pound using a mortar and pestle. Transfer to a sealed jar and refrigerate. The paste will keep for up to 6 months.

jt's vinaigrette

Use this as a dressing for all leafy salads and for cold roasted vegetables.

makes 400ml/14fl oz/1¾ cups
1 tbsp Dijon mustard
75ml/2½fl oz/5 tbsp red wine vinegar
1 tsp walnut oil
300ml/½ pint/1¼ cups extra virgin olive oil
sea salt
freshly ground black pepper

method

Place the mustard and vinegar in a bowl and whisk until blended. Slowly add the walnut and olive oils, still whisking, and season with salt and freshly ground black pepper to taste. The dressing will keep for up to 1 month in an airtight jar.

yellow curry paste

The basis of many Thai curries, this paste gives a distinctive colour and flavour.

makes 500ml/17fl oz/generous 2 cups
250g/8oz long yellow chillies, deseeded and chopped
6 Thai shallots, chopped
5 lime leaves, torn
3 garlic cloves, chopped
60g/2oz galangal, peeled and chopped
2 tsp salt
1 tsp shrimp paste
30g/1oz dried shrimps
30g/1oz fresh turmeric root, chopped

method

Place all the ingredients in the bowl of a food processor and process to a fine paste. Alternatively, pound using a mortar and pestle. Transfer to a sealed jar and then refrigerate. The paste will keep for up to 6 months.

pesto

makes 500ml/17fl oz/generous 2 cups
125g/4oz basil
75g/2½oz flat-leaf parsley, leaves only
125g/4oz pine nuts
3 garlic cloves
500ml/17fl oz/generous 2 cups extra virgin olive oil
125g/4oz freshly grated Parmesan
sea salt
freshly ground black pepper

method

Place the herbs, pine nuts and garlic in the bowl of a food processor, and process to a rough paste. On a medium speed, slowly add the olive oil until it forms a smooth emulsion, then stir in the Parmesan. Season to taste and store in an airtight container for up to 1 month.

asian pesto

A more fragrant Asian version of Italian pesto, this is served with noodles or roasted vegetables.

makes 300ml/½ pint/1¼ cups
200g/7oz coriander, roots left on
45g/1½oz mint
45g/1½oz unsalted roasted peanuts
2 tbsp freshly squeezed lime juice
4 garlic cloves
250ml/8fl oz/1 cup olive oil
sea salt
freshly ground black pepper

method

Place the herbs, peanuts, lime juice and garlic in the bowl of a food processor. At medium speed, slowly drizzle the olive oil into the mixture, until it forms a smooth paste. Season to taste. Transfer to an airtight container and refrigerate. It will keep for up to 3 months.

pistou

Use to add flavour to soups or fish.

makes 300ml/½ pint/1¼ cups
9 sprigs basil
9 garlic cloves, crushed
250ml/8fl oz/1 cup olive oil
125g/4oz/1 cup freshly grated Parmesan

method

Place the basil and garlic in the bowl of a food processor. On medium speed, slowly add the olive oil until you have a smooth paste. Stir in the Parmesan and transfer to an airtight jar. Store in the refrigerator. Pistou will keep for up to 1 month.

salsa verde

Serve with fish or vegetable dishes.

makes 400ml/14fl oz/1¾ cups
60g/2oz watercress
60g/2oz spinach
60g/2oz flat-leaf parsley
60g/2oz tarragon
60g/2oz chervil
2 sprigs basil
1 garlic clove
375ml/12fl oz/1½ cups mayonnaise
60ml/2fl oz/¼ cup double cream
sea salt
freshly ground black pepper

method

Place the watercress, spinach, herbs and garlic in the bowl of a food processor, and process to a purée. Stir in the mayonnaise and cream to thin to pouring consistency. Season to taste. Use within 3 days.

deep-fried spring onions

makes 30g/1oz/1 cup
600ml/1 pint/2½ cups vegetable oil
8 spring onions, cut lengthwise as finely as possible

method

Heat the oil until shimmering, then drop in the shredded spring onions, taking care to stand back as the oil will spit, and fry for 30–40 seconds. Remove the fried onions with a slotted spoon and drain on paper towels.

deep-fried chillies, shallots and garlic

Use as a garnish, scattered on spicy stir-fries and curries.

makes 90g/3oz/1½ cups
250ml/8fl oz/1 cup peanut oil
6 Thai shallots, sliced lengthwise
8 garlic cloves, sliced lengthwise
6 red chillies, deseeded and sliced

method

Heat the oil in a pan over a moderate heat and deep-fry the shallots until golden. Remove with a slotted spoon and drain on paper towels. Reheat the oil and deep-fry the garlic. Again remove with a slotted spoon and drain on paper towels. Repeat with the chillies, and drain well. It is important always to deep-fry in this order, otherwise the oil will become too highly flavoured.

preserved lemons

Stir into rice or cous cous dishes to give an authentic Middle Eastern flavour.

makes 1 litre/1¾ pints/4 cups
4 firm medium lemons
100g/3½oz/⅓ cup fine sea salt
7cm/3in cinnamon stick
2 tsp coriander seeds
1 tsp black peppercorns
4 whole cloves
750ml/1¼ pints/3 cups water

method

Bring a large pan of water to the boil and add the lemons. Return to the boil and simmer for 3 minutes. Transfer the lemons to a bowl of cold water and refresh, then drain and pat dry on paper towels. Place the salt, cinnamon stick, coriander seeds, peppercorns and cloves in a pan and add the measured water. Bring to the boil. Cut the lemons into quarters, top to bottom, leaving the quarters attached at the base. Place in a large sterilized jar and pour over the boiling hot spice mixture to cover, including the cinnamon stick, and seal. This will keep for up to 6 months.

salted duck eggs

Delicious used for Deep-fried Eggs with Sweet Fish Sauce (page 46) or chopped up and served with noodles.

makes 10 eggs
750ml/1¼ pints/3 cups water
300g/10oz/1 cup sea salt
10 fresh duck eggs

method

Bring the water to the boil over a moderate heat and add the salt, stirring to ensure it is fully dissolved. Allow to cool. Place the eggs in a large preserving jar, or plastic container with a lid, and pour over the cold salt solution. Seal and date, and store in the refrigerator for 4 weeks. When ready to use, remove from the salt water and drain.

pasta

makes 500g/1lb
325g/11oz/2¾ cups '00' pasta flour,
   plus extra for dusting
½ tsp sea salt
3 medium eggs
1 medium egg yolk
2 tsp olive oil

method

Place the flour and salt in the bowl of a food processor. Add 2 eggs and process to blend. Add the remaining egg and egg yolk and process again. Add the olive oil, with the machine still running. The mixture should have a texture resembling breadcrumbs. Remove from the bowl and place on a lightly floured work surface. Gently knead to form a rough dough, about 1–2 minutes. The dough should be crumbly but hold together. If it is too dry, add a little water on your fingertips. Wrap in clingfilm and refrigerate for at least 2 hours. Roll out using a pasta machine, or by hand.

polenta

makes 750g/1½lb/3 cups
250ml/8fl oz/1 cup water
300ml/½ pint/1¼ cups milk
¼ tsp sea salt
¼ tsp freshly ground black pepper
1 garlic clove, crushed
125g/4oz/⅔ cup instant polenta
125ml/4fl oz/½ cup double cream
30g/1oz/¼ cup freshly grated Parmesan
75g/2½oz mascarpone

method

Place half the water and half the milk in a pan over a high heat. Add the salt, pepper and garlic and bring to the boil. Mix the remaining milk and water in a small bowl and stir in the polenta, whisking to a thin paste. Add the polenta mixture to the boiling liquid (it must be boiling or the polenta will become lumpy), stirring constantly. Return the pan to the boil, and then lower the heat and cook for 45 minutes, stirring frequently, until the polenta is white and creamy, and the garlic has dissolved. Add the cream and Parmesan and stir until combined, then remove from the heat and stir in the mascarpone.

pizza dough

This dough makes a perfect base for Pissaladière (page 158).

makes 1 x 30cm/12in pizza base
2 tsp fresh yeast, or 1 tsp dried yeast
1 tsp caster sugar
60ml/2fl oz/¼ cup warm water
250g/8oz/2 cups '00' bread flour, plus
   extra for dusting
1 tbsp olive oil
2 tsp fine sea salt

method

Combine the yeast, sugar and half the water in a small bowl and set aside for 5 minutes until frothy. Sift the flour 3 times into a large bowl, pour over the olive oil, and rub in with your fingertips. Leave in a warm place for 30 minutes. Add the yeast mixture to the remaining water, and stir in well. Mix in the salt with the warmed flour and olive oil, and gently incorporate the yeast liquid, adding a little extra water if the dough is too dry. Knead on a floured board for 4–5 minutes, then cover with a damp cloth and leave in a warm place to rest for 30 minutes, or until doubled in size. Roll out into a large circle about 30cm/12in in diameter, and place on a floured baking tray.

puff pastry

Lighter than short pastries, but with a much richer, buttery taste, puff pastry is used for delicate patisseries and tarts. The ready-made, frozen variety is never very satisfactory, so although it is time-consuming to make your own, it is well worth the effort.

makes 1kg/2lb
500g/1lb/4 cups plain flour, plus extra for dusting
pinch of salt
375g/12oz/1½ cups unsalted butter
200ml/7fl oz/scant 1 cup water
2 tsp lemon juice

method

Sift the flour and salt into a bowl. Take 60g/2oz/ ¼ cup of the butter and chill the remainder. Rub the butter into the flour with your fingertips until the mixture is like fine breadcrumbs. Make a well in the centre, pour in the water and lemon juice, and slowly work into the dry ingredients until you have a smooth dough. Shape into a ball, cover with clingfilm, and rest in the refrigerator for 1 hour.

   Place the dough on a floured board and score a cross in the top of the ball. Roll out the dough in 4 directions until it forms a fat cross. Soften the chilled butter by pounding it several times with a rolling pin, then place the block in the centre of the cross. Fold the 'arms' of the cross over the butter, so it is completely concealed, and rest the dough in the refrigerator for 30 minutes.

   Transfer the dough to a floured board and roll out into a long rectangle, about 70 x 30cm/28 x 12in. Mark into thirds. Fold the top third of the strip downwards, and the bottom third upwards, to create 3 layers. Give the dough a quarter turn clockwise, and repeat the rolling and folding. This is called the first turn. Wrap the dough in clingfilm and rest in the refrigerator for 30 minutes. Repeat the rolling and folding process 2 more times, giving the dough a quarter turn each time so that the fold is always on the right. Rest in the refrigerator for a final 30 minutes. The pastry is now ready for use.

shortcrust pastry

makes enough for one pastry case
23cm/9in in diameter
250g/8oz/2 cups plain flour
125g/4oz/½ cup unsalted butter
pinch of salt
1 medium egg yolk
60ml/2fl oz/¼ cup iced water

method

Sift the flour into a bowl and add the butter and salt. Using a knife, rather than your fingers, cut together the flour, butter and salt until you have a texture resembling breadcrumbs (this takes more time, but ensures the pastry remains cool, which helps prevent it from shrinking when baked). Alternatively, use a pulse-action food processor. Stir in the egg yolk and water, bringing the mixture together into a crumbly dough. Shape into a ball, wrap in clingfilm and rest in the refrigerator for at least 1 hour, preferably overnight. Roll out to the required size, allowing a little extra for shrinkage, and chill for another 30 minutes before baking.

sweet shortcrust pastry

makes enough for one pastry case
23cm/9in in diameter
250g/8oz/2 cups plain flour
175g/6oz/¾ cup unsalted butter
90g/3oz/⅓ cup caster sugar
zest of ¼ lemon
1 large egg

method

Sift the flour into a bowl, add the butter and rub in with your fingertips until it looks like fine breadcrumbs. Stir in the sugar and lemon zest. Make a well in the centre and add the egg, working it into the flour with your fingertips. Shape the dough into a ball, wrap in clingfilm and rest in the refrigerator for 30 minutes. Roll out to the required size, allowing a little extra for shrinkage, and chill for another 30 minutes before baking.

vanilla sugar

makes 500g/1lb/2 cups
5 vanilla pods
500g/1lb/2 cups caster sugar

method

Lie the vanilla pods flat, and tie both ends together. Push the two ends of the bunch together, so that the pods fold like a concertina, and place in a jar with the caster sugar. Leave for at least 4–5 days before using. Vanilla sugar keeps indefinitely, and the jar can be topped up with extra sugar as it is used, for as long as the vanilla pods remain fragrant.

ginger juice

This gives a concentrated ginger flavour to buns and sauces.

makes about 125ml/4fl oz/½ cup
60g/2oz fresh root ginger, peeled and roughly chopped
small bowl of lukewarm water

method

Wrap the chopped ginger in a piece of muslin, and drop into the bowl of warm water. Leave for 4–5 minutes, then remove the ginger and squeeze the juices from the muslin bag into an empty bowl. Repeat a second time, then discard the muslin bag. The squeezed liquid is ginger juice.

tamarind water

Use to give a distinctive sour flavour to Thai and Asian soups and curries.

makes 125ml/4fl oz/½ cup
90g/3oz tamarind pulp, dried or compressed, available from Asian grocers or supermarkets
175ml/6fl oz/¾ cup lukewarm water

method

Place the tamarind pulp in a bowl, and cover with the water. With the back of a fork, crush the tamarind slightly, and leave to stand for 30 minutes. Drain off the water through a fine sieve and discard the pulp. Thick tamarind water is made with less liquid, and the pulp is crushed harder to create a darker water.

custard

Delicious both hot and cold, custard is the perfect accompaniment to puddings.

makes 500ml/17fl oz/generous 2 cups
250ml/8fl oz/1 cup full-cream milk
250ml/8fl oz/1 cup single cream
5 egg yolks
1 vanilla pod
75g/2½oz/5 tbsp caster sugar

method

Bring a pan of water to the boil. Alternatively, use a double boiler. Place the milk, cream and yolks in a bowl and whisk until amalgamated. Set the bowl on top of the pan of boiling water, add the vanilla pod and bring to a gentle simmer, whisking continuously. Mix in the sugar and continue to simmer, whisking, until the custard begins the thicken, 3–4 minutes. Remove from the heat, take out the vanilla pod (this can be re-used) and pour through a conical sieve to remove any cooked egg. Either refrigerate for later use, or return to the bowl over the pan, warm through, and serve.

roast peking duck

Peking ducks can be bought fresh, frozen or even ready-roasted, in Chinese supermarkets. Do not substitute English ducks, or any other kind of duck, as they are much fatter under the skin, and hence less crisp when cooked.

1 Peking duck
150g/5oz/⅔ cup sugar
1 cinnamon stick, broken into pieces
5 star anise
12cm/5in piece root ginger, peeled and sliced
3 spring onions, roughly chopped
2 tbsp red Chinese vinegar
2 tbsp maltose (page 12)
1 tbsp water

method

Rinse the duck thoroughly under cold running water. Drain well and pat dry with paper towels.

Mix together the sugar, cinnamon stick, star anise, ginger and spring onions, and place in the cavity of the duck. Secure the vent with a wooden skewer (pre-soaked to prevent it splintering) to hold the stuffing in place. Boil a kettle full of water. Score the skin of the duck with a Chinese cleaver and pour the boiling water over the bird.

Place the vinegar, maltose and 1 tablespoonful of water in a small pan and bring to the boil. Place the duck on a wire rack over a roasting tin and spoon over the hot liquid. Hook the duck through the neck and hang it up overnight to allow the maltose to be absorbed into the skin. Alternatively, leave on the wire rack and place in the refrigerator overnight.

Preheat the oven to 220°C/425°F/Gas 7. Place the duck on a rack over a roasting tin containing 125ml/4fl oz/1 cup of water and roast on the top shelf for 35–40 minutes, until the skin is dark and crispy. Remove from the oven and allow to rest for 30 minutes.

boning roast duck

Place the roast duck breast-side down on a board and, using a sharp cleaver or knife, score the skin to the left and right of the backbone. Turn breast-side up, and repeat the cut to the left and right of the breastbone, cutting on to the ribs and using the meat's own weight to ease it free. Slice through the bone that separates the breast and neck at each side and, using the flat of the cleaver, peel the breast away from the backbone, so that one half of the duck is removed.

Repeat with the other side and, squeezing the meat back into shape, place on a baking sheet. Add the thighs and wings, removed by running the cleaver along the skin side of the bone and twisting the meat free. The duck is now boned.

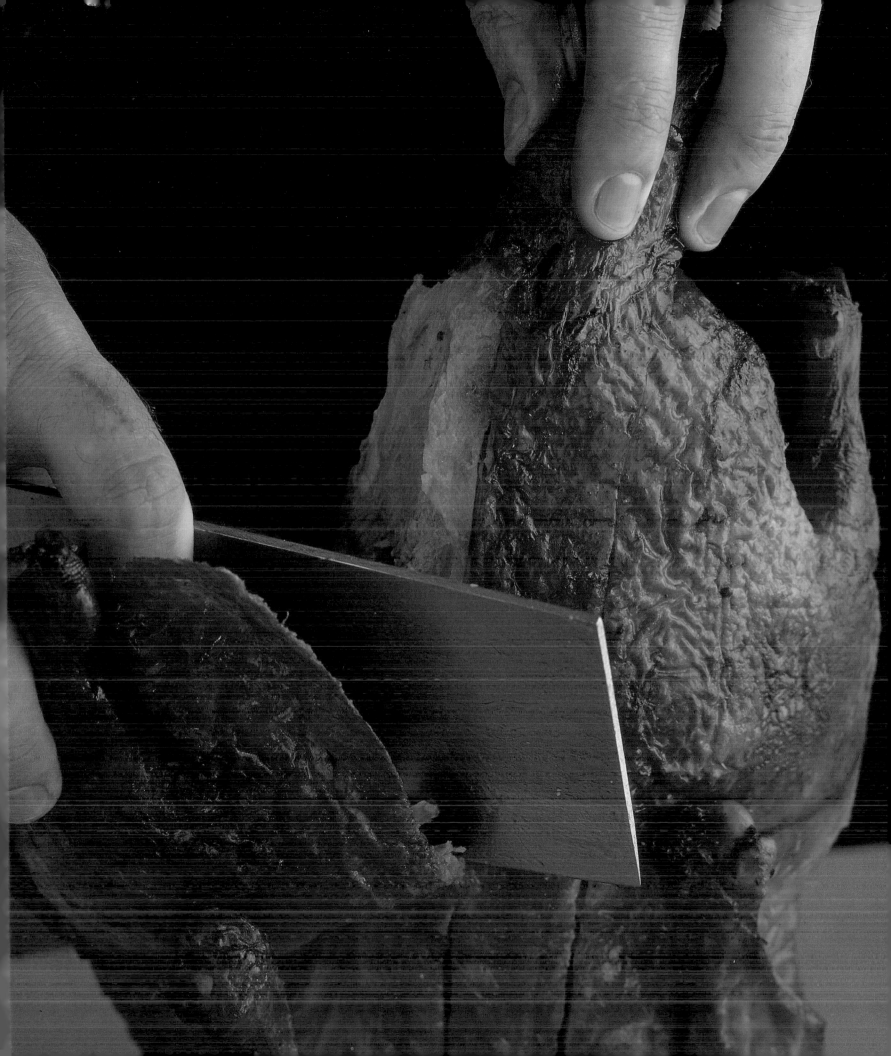

bain-marie

A shallow pan or tray filled with boiling water in which bowls or dishes containing delicate puddings such as custards are placed for gentle cooking in the oven. Similar in principle to the American double boiler, a bain-marie prevents food from drying out or cooking too fast, as the heat is kept at a constant temperature. The water should not be allowed to come more than half-way up the sides of the bowls.

bake blind

A method of part-cooking a pastry shell so that the pastry is crisp before being filled, thus preventing it from going soggy. To bake blind, line a flan tin with pastry then cover with foil or greaseproof paper. Fill with baking beans or rice and cook in a hot oven for about 10–15 minutes. Remove the beans and the paper about three-quarters of the way through cooking to allow the pastry to dry out. Remove from the oven. While still hot, brush the tart case with raw egg white. The egg will cook and seal the tart, ensuring that no filling runs out.

braise

The application of heat to a closed or hermetically sealed container or cooking vessel made of steel, terracotta, glass or cast iron. Braising is a slow cooking method used for larger items such as beef shin, pork belly and root vegetables. Because the food is cooked in its own juices, the flavours are retained, and even tougher meat joints become tender if cooked for a long period in this way.

caramelize

To turn sugar into caramel by gently heating. Caramel can be made by heating sugar or a sugar syrup – the latter is preferable as syrup is less likely to burn. There are many degrees of caramel, from very dark to very light. All need great care due to the intensity of heat (the sugar reaches a temperature of almost 200°C/400°F). To stop caramel cooking, plunge the base of the pan into cold water. When cooked gently, the sugars in vegetables and fruit also caramelize, resulting in a glazed or coloured appearance, e.g. caramelized onions.

cartouche

A piece of stiff paper cut into a circle the same diameter as a cooking pan, with a hole in the centre. It is used as a cover when cooking items in liquid to ensure the food does not rise up above the surface whilst allowing the steam to dissipate.

cleaver

The Chinese use a large cleaver (shaped like a small axe) for chopping and slicing meat and vegetables. It is also used for boning Peking duck (page 218).

deep-fry

To cook food by immersing it in very hot fat or oil. This is usually done in a specially designed deep-fryer, although a wok or deep pan can also be used. The object is to seal the outside of the food quickly, locking in the flavour and allowing the centre to steam, resulting in a crisp surface and a moist inside. Deep-fried food is sometimes coated first in egg, batter or breadcrumbs, to protect tender items from the heat.

griddle

A cast-iron plate used for grilling (see below).

grill

The application of heat to food placed directly above or below. The heat can be directed by means of a metal griddle plate or bars, and the heat source can be a gas flame, electricity or burning wood or charcoal. A fast cooking method, grilling is used primarily for cooking slabs or slices of meat, fish and vegetables. The food usually needs to be turned a few times during the cooking process to ensure an even colour. The American term 'broil' usually refers to the application of heat from above. This method of cooking is slower than using a griddle, and does not result in such intensity of flavour.

julienne

In classic cookery, a piece of vegetable cut into thin strips approximately 5cm x 5mm/2 x ¼in. The recipes in this book allow for julienne strips to be

suppliers

The organizations, shops and markets listed have been selected to provide a helpful starting point in tracking down quality food outlets and specialist stores.

UK
Henrietta Green's *Food Lovers' Guide to Britain, 1996–97* (BBC Books, £12.99) provides a comprehensive list of quality producers in the UK.

The National Federation of Fishmongers
(advises on quality fishmongers)
Pisces, London Road
Feering
Colchester CO5 9ED
Tel: (01376) 571 391

Billingsgate Fish Market
Trafalgar Way
Poplar
London E14 5ST

The Q Guild of Butchers
(advises on quality butchers)
Winter Hill House
Snowdon Drive
Milton Keynes MK6 1AX
Tel: (01908) 235018

The Oil Merchant
(mail order)
47 Ashchurch Grove
London W12 9BU
Tel: (0181) 740 1335

Wild Harvest *(mushrooms)*
31 London Stone Estate
Broughton
London SW8 3QJ
Tel: (0171) 498 5397

The Soil Association
(produces a list of organic suppliers)
86 Colston Street
Bristol BS1 5BB
Tel: (0117) 929 0661

Winner Foods
(advises on Asian food outlets)
Unit B 43–53 Markfield Road
London N15 4QA
Tel: (0171) 880 3678

Loong Fung Supermarket
42–44 Gerrard Street
London W1V 7LP
Tel: (0171) 437 7332

USA
American Meat Institute (AMI)
(advises on quality butchers)
PO Box 3556
Washington, DC 20007
Tel: (703) 841 2400

Produce Marketing Association
(advises on outlets for specific ingredients)
1500 Casho Mill Road
PO Box 6036
Newark, DE 19714–6036,
Tel: (302) 738 7100

Farm Verified Organic
(produces a list of organic suppliers)
RR1, Box 40A
Medina, ND 58467
Tel: (701) 486 3578

AUSTRALIA
Sydney Fish Market
Pyrmont

Toofey's Fishmonger
Carlton
Melbourne

Paddy's Markets
Newfarm, Brisbane and
Sydney

Leichardt Market
Sydney

Queen Victoria Market
Melbourne

South Melbourne Market
Melbourne

Prahran Market
South Yarra

Rock and Roll Deli
Greenslopes
Brisbane

David Jones Department Stores
Melbourne and Sydney

The Vital Ingredient
South Melbourne

Simon Johnson Purveyor of
Fine Foods
Fitzroy, Melbourne and
Pyrmont, Sydney

Black Pearl Caviar
Speciality Foods
Fortitude Valley
Brisbane

NEW ZEALAND
New Zealand Meat
Producers' Board
(advises on quality butchers)
110 Featherston Street
PO Box 121
Wellington
Tel: 0–4–473 9150

New Zealand Fishing
Industry Board
(advises on quality fishmongers)
Private Bag 24091
Manners Street Post Office
74 Cambridge Terrace
Wellington
Tel: 0–4–385 4005

Herb Federation of New
Zealand
PO Box 20–002
Te Rapa
Hamilton
Tel: 0–7–308 9088

author's acknowledgments

Our grateful thanks to Bruce Hyman, for fighting, and winning, the many battles which have made this book what it is; to Tim Peplow and Jonathan Raimes at Foundation Graphic Co for creating a tangible product out of a lot of vague ideas and arguments; to James Murphy, Diana Miller and Wei Tang, whose beautiful photography and patient reworkings were an inspiration from beginning to end (not to mention James' 26 bottles of red wine); to Kate Bell, Suzannah Gough and Helen Lewis at Conran Octopus, for their constant enthusiasm and months of hard work; to the opening crew at Mezzo, (and in particular, David Loewi, Chris Galvin, Graham Harris, Wendy Henricks, Sally McCausland and Andy Smith), without whose slavish efforts and ongoing commitment there would be no restaurant about which to write this book; to the great and good people who every day work their butts off to ensure that standards are maintained and that Mezzo continues to flourish, especially Tom Meenaghan, Richard Lee, Darren Farr and Jason Warwick; to Simon Wright, for his guidance and invaluable judgement; to Trinka Smith and Lucy Laidlow, who each, in the midst of daily chaos and indecipherable faxes, managed to keep things running smoothly; to Simon Willis, for his hard work and long negotiations; to Terence Conran, whose vision, energy and direction were the motivations around which this book was written; and lastly, to Angie Torode, for putting up with a husband who never arrives home when he says he will, and when he does, has 200 pages of proofs under his arm to correct before the next day.

publisher's acknowledgments

The publishers would like to thank Tracey Beresford, Hilary Bird, The Conran Shop, Leslie Harrington and Jane Royston for their invaluable assistance.